Law and practice
in
chattel secured farm credit

Law and practice
in
chattel secured farm credit

GLENN R. COATES

The University of Wisconsin Press

Madison, 1954

Published by the University of Wisconsin Press,
811 State Street, Madison, Wisconsin

Copyright, 1954, by the Regents of the University of Wisconsin
Copyright, Canada, 1954
Distributed in Canada by Burns and MacEachern, Toronto

Printed in the United States of America
by Vail-Ballou Press, Incorporated, Binghamton, New York

Library of Congress Catalogue Card Number 54-6742

PREFACE

Legal scholars have devoted considerable thought and effort in recent years to the impact of law on the economic life and social order of our society. Yet even at this date we actually know very little about the role of law as it affects the behavior of the groups regulated by it.

This study attempts to make a contribution to such knowledge by giving special attention to the effect of law in a selected field. It reports and discusses the legal ramifications of a business transaction which closely affects the Wisconsin farm economy. This transaction is the granting of a loan by a bank or other private credit institution to a Wisconsin farmer and the securing of that loan with the farmer's chattel property. It is a transaction which for the most part comes into existence and is followed through to conclusion without the aid of a lawyer; yet, clearly, the transaction is clothed in legal documents, and the rights and remedies of both parties are affected by the law as it has been set forth in court decisions and legislative enactments.

This study emphasizes the manner and degree that farm loans are promoted or hindered, as the case may be, by relevant court decisions and legislative enactments. It attempts to determine just how this body of law affects the behavior of businessmen, particularly those who make a business of financing the farmer. Thus it departs from the traditional emphasis on the structure of legal rules as such.

This approach I consider basic in any "law in action" research. If we accept the proposition that law exists not for itself but in the interest of a well-ordered society then it is important to know the patterns of action which have developed in the area supposedly ordered by a particular rule of law. I have therefore attempted to ascertain the action taken to conform to a particular rule of law, the efforts made to circumvent that rule when it blocks a desired end, and, finally, the patterns established by those who are uninformed or misinformed about that rule.

But a mere reporting of the behavior of a particular group under the law and the effects of the law on the group is not the sole objective of this approach. Inevitable results of a study such as this are indications of how business behavior should and does influence law. Any piece of legislation and any court decision should be grounded to the business facts relative to the issue in question. The modern farm economy cannot continue to operate under legal rules designed and promulgated to fit another day. To the extent that business behavior has departed from legal rules, lawyers and legislators must in many instances recognize the departure as a necessary result of a changing attitude. In some instances the law must "catch up" if it is to do its job.

This criticism implies a definition of law in the narrow sense of court decisions and legislative enactments. In the larger and truer sense, the "living law" does keep pace, and its effect is and should be felt. This study recognizes that law has more than one significant meaning. Law means what the courts have said in numerous reported decisions, and it means also what legislators have said in statutes designed to clarify, expand, or change those court decisions.

But if those were the only meanings, I should have conducted my entire research in a law library. I should have simply read every case and statute involving secured transactions. Instead, I recognized that in addition to court decisions and state statutes the law affecting chattel secured loans means what the chattel mortgage form, the conditional sales form, and the assignment form, to name only a few of the chattel loan instruments, say about the rights and remedies of the parties; it means what the lender understands it to mean and what the borrower understands it to mean. I recognized also that this understanding in turn may vary in accordance with what their respective attorneys have told the lender and the borrower.

MY SOURCES of information on existing practices were the bankers, the lawyers, and the loan company managers throughout Wisconsin. This book would not have been possible without their splendid cooperation.

I should also like to thank Professor J. H. Beuscher, of the University of Wisconsin Law School, for his helpful suggestions throughout the course of my research. He served as an excellent sounding board for the development of each idea, and our conferences after each series of interviews did much to give meaning to a mass of information.

The considerable material on the proposed Uniform Commercial Code was derived from the sincere and constant cooperation of Professor Charles Bunn, also of the University of Wisconsin Law School. He gave freely of his time to discuss with me the latest drafts and their intended effect on the problems under consideration.

To the extent that the material is readable by being free of legalisms, the reader has my wife to thank. To her fell the thankless task of typing the manuscript and then reading it for clarity and readability.

Grateful acknowledgment also is due the Carnegie Corporation of New York for the necessary funds to support this study, including the many trips throughout the state for firsthand information.

GLENN R. COATES

Racine, Wisconsin
November, 1953

CONTENTS

ix

CHAPTER THREE

Policing and Administering
Secured Loans—Rights
of Third Parties

CHAPTER FOUR

Enforcement of the Security
Where Debtor Defaults

CHAPTER FIVE

Theory and Effect of Existing Law
of Chattel Secured Farm Credit

Law and practice
in
chattel secured farm credit

CHAPTER ONE

Introduction

1. THE LAW OF SECURED TRANSACTIONS

The law of secured transactions as established by the court and legislature serves the dual purpose of resolving conflicts and protecting us from ourselves. For example, many of the court decisions on the subject are concerned with a determination of those farm assets which can be the subject of a secured transaction and with a consideration of the effects the creation and existence of that transaction might have on the subsequent use of those assets by the farmer. For this reason we have the court-made rule that property has to be in existence and owned by the farmer before that property can be mortgaged to the lender. The theoretical basis of the court rule is, as we shall note in detail later, the maxim, "a man cannot grant which he hath not." From a social and economic viewpoint, the court probably feels that such a rule is desirable because it prevents a borrower from overextending his credit in that he is prevented from encumbering his assets far in advance of acquiring them. If the lender takes an interest in future goods as security, the interest is void.

There is also the court-made rule that a debtor may not sell or otherwise dispose of the encumbered asset even though the act is done with the consent of the creditor. The theoretical basis of this rule is that such free and easy dealing would be a fraud on other creditors. The social reason is, probably, that a hard and fast rule declaring such consent on the part of the lender the equivalent of waiving the mortgage would in effect make it easier to resolve conflicts between prior and subsequent lenders and purchasers. The hard and fast rule avoids the necessity of actually proving and finding fraud.

To a lawyer, the rules set forth seem to be fixed and workable in spite of certain obvious difficulties of deciding when a crop or a new born calf comes into existence. But those problems can be met and solved on a case-to-case basis because the overriding principles are definite. To a farmer, however, the overriding principles present objectionable features. How, for example, can he get a loan to buy seed when the security to be offered is the crop to be grown? Or how can he get a loan to buy a dairy cow and offer the cow as security on a mortgage? In neither case is the asset owned (or in existence) at the time of the loan. Or how can he weed out poor producers from his dairy herd and buy better cattle if the poor producer is on a mortgage which by court rule restricts his power to sell or dispose of the asset?

The Wisconsin legislators, insofar as they have expressed themselves by statutes in this field, have been concerned with fixing the procedure whereby the lender could realize repayment of the loan by a sale of the security in the event it became necessary and, further, with establishing a requirement of placing the security document on public record. This requirement is a method of protecting the first lender's interest from other lenders or from purchasers of the secured asset. In effect the legislature told the first lender to inform the public that he claimed rights against the secured asset by placing the legal document giving him those rights on file with a county official. The legislature went on to provide that if the first lender did not do so, those rights would be invalid against another lender or purchaser later in time. In the absence of such statute the court would have protected the first lender on the legal theory that the debtor had nothing to give the second lender.[1] Again, this statutory rule facilitated the solution of conflicts between various parties claiming an interest in the security.

The other principal statutory rule has the avowed purpose of protecting the debtor against the unscrupulous lender. It provides a fixed procedure whereby the lender can realize on his security if it becomes necessary. The procedure is clothed with restrictions on the activities of the lender. Notice of the foreclosure sale must be given to the debtor in ample time for him to refinance. The sale must be public if the debtor so demands. This provision presumably assures the debtor of the highest price for his assets and thereby reduces a possible claim for a deficiency. The theory of such protection is adopted from the rules which courts of equity have from the beginning applied to protect the real estate mortgage debtor from losing his land without an opportunity to refinance or recover from a period of reverses.

In establishing these rules the legislature has expanded, clarified, and to a degree changed the court-made rules. But the rules and regulations seem to have had very little effect on the desired end of facilitating the financing of agriculture by chattel secured credit. The question therefore suggests itself: If the principles which govern chattel secured farm credit in Wisconsin do not adequately encourage and facilitate agricultural production, are there sound reasons for their continued pronouncement by the court and support by the legislature?

The rule that a mortgage on property not then owned by the debtor is invalid was initially set forth by the court in the short opinion, *Comstock* v. *Scales*.[2] Authority for the rule was placed on *The Bank of Lansingburgh* v. *Crary*[3] and *Otis* v. *Sill*.[4] This rule in Wisconsin was later expanded in *Chynoweth* v. *Tenney*,[5] which cited *Lunn* v. *Thornton*.[6] A review of these cases shows a reliance on the maxim, "a man cannot grant or charge that which he hath not." Historically this maxim may have been valid when the passing of legal title depended upon delivery of the thing. In such cases if a man wanted to grant or convey a chattel he did it by actual delivery; if he wanted to grant land he passed a twig or a handful of soil to symbolize the act. This act of delivery was attended with much ceremony by witnesses who established the fact that the delivery had been complete. But how much application does the maxim have in the modern secured loan transaction? If the lender wishes to loan money and take as security the cattle which are to be purchased with that money and the borrower wishes to have the loan and is willing to offer the cattle as security, should this maxim prevent them from doing so?

The rule that a chattel mortgage is void if the lender grants

authority to the debtor to sell or otherwise dispose of the goods
has as its foundation two expressed reasons: (1) that such authority is inconsistent with the theory of a mortgage, and (2) that it is
a fraud on other creditors.[7] The court in asserting the inconsistency
of such authority was probably thinking in terms of a single asset,
legal title to which has passed to the lender by virtue of the mortgage. If the debtor fails to repay the loan, the lender may take
possession of the asset and sell it to satisfy the obligation. Granting
authority to the debtor to sell the asset would then be contrary
to the purpose of the security aspects of the transaction. It is suggested, however, that if we think in terms of the farmer's inventory
—his machinery or his herd of cattle—and recognize that increas-
ing his capacity to produce will increase his chances of repaying
the loan, there is nothing inconsistent in permitting him to exchange certain of his inventory as good management dictates. It
is further suggested that there is little economic risk to the lender
in such freedom of exchange as long as he continues to grant loans
on the ability of the farmer to repay rather than on just the collateral offered.

In asserting that such authority is a fraud on other creditors,
the court was presumably recognizing the possibility that a friendly
creditor might arrange for a mortgage on all the debtor's assets.
Because of the mortgage, unsecured creditors would be in a less
advantageous position for collecting their claims, since there would
be no property free and clear and thus subject to levy. Meanwhile
the friendly mortgagee would permit the debtor to sell the assets
and use the proceeds. This argument cannot be lightly dismissed.
It is incumbent upon any legal system to remedy such an obvious
wrong. It is suggested, however, that the court should look behind
the facts to ascertain if these conditions do exist instead of declaring the mortgage void at the outset because the authority for
such action is there. In other words, fraud should not be presumed;
it should be alleged and proved by the unsecured debtor. It is possible that proof of fraud may be difficult to obtain in some cases,
but the value to farm economy of legal freedom to exchange farm
assets far outweighs occasional harm to the creditor.

As has been noted, the principal contributions of the legislature
in this field are provisions for public record of the security interest
and for foreclosure. These provisions are designed to resolve con-

flicts between various lenders who have claims against the same debtor and to protect the debtor from oppression.[8]

The foreclosure remedy is seldom used. In many cases arrangements are made whereby the debtor sells the mortgaged property himself and delivers the proceeds to the lender. In other cases the debtor voluntarily delivers the goods to the lender who sells them privately and retains the proceeds. The filing provision is also not followed as religiously as might be expected. This provision in effect tells the first lender to place his document on record or run the risk of losing his secured position to a purchaser or mortgagee subsequent in time. The larger credit institutions have found that on a volume basis it is less expensive to insure against this risk with a private insurance company than it is to pay the filing fee on each document. This fact does not and is not intended to reflect on the wisdom of a provision for public recordation of security rights.

However, as far as the strict foreclosure provisions are concerned the fact that they have fallen into general disuse indicates certain shortcomings in the system. There is certainly some thinking that the public foreclosure sale not only does not attract the best price but is limited to the bargain hunters. In fact, more often than not the only attendant at the sale is the lender, whose bid is the only one made. Yet the legislation is designed to protect the borrower from having to accept the lender's price. There is no evidence of oppression in fact on the part of the lender, particularly when a reputable firm is involved. All available evidence points to close cooperation by the debtor with the creditor in resolving the defaulted debt to their mutual advantage. This suggests that the debtor believes that his interest is promoted by a private sale of the assets on the commercial market rather than at public sale.

2. Secured credit instruments

A word should be said at this point about the various secured credit instruments in use in Wisconsin. The situations in which they are used and the manner of use will be discussed in considerable detail in the following chapters.

The most popular device in use is the chattel mortgage. Under this arrangement the lender makes a loan to the borrower who signs a note by which he promises to repay the loan over a fixed period of time, usually by amortization based on the month or pay periods. In addition to the note the borrower gives the lender a chattel mortgage on all or certain selected personal property which the borrower owns and possesses at the time of the mortgage. In theory, title to the property passes by virtue of the mortgage to the lender.[9] However, possession can and usually does remain in the borrower. In the event that the borrower defaults in payments, or in the event that the lender otherwise considers the debt insecure, the lender has the right of immediate possession of the goods covered by his mortgage. He may then sell the goods to satisfy the indebtedness. Statutes govern the latter procedure.

A second device in widespread use is the conditional sales contract. This device contemplates a contract to sell a chattel by the vendor to the purchaser. The purchaser agrees to pay for the chattel in regular payments and takes possession of the chattel. The vendor meanwhile retains legal title to the chattel to secure the payment of the purchase price. In the event that the purchaser fails to make the prescribed payments, the vendor has a right to take possession of the chattel and to hold it or sell it, depending upon the total of payments made by the purchaser. Statutes again govern the method of sale.

For the most part, banks prefer chattel mortgage arrangements, while auction finance companies prefer the conditional sales contract. Certain reasons for this arise out of the nature of the respective documents.

The conditional sales contract by its terms contemplates a sale with deferred payments. The contract initially is between the vendor and purchaser. The credit institution comes into the picture only by a purchase of the contract from the vendor without any prior contact with the debtor-purchaser. Banks place great emphasis on the character of the borrower and desire a complete discussion of his financial picture at the time the loan is made. The security is of secondary importance. On the other hand the finance company or auction sale company deals with a poorer risk at higher rates and thus places more emphasis on the security itself.

Moreover, banks prefer to encumber much or all of the farm personal property when making a farm loan, regardless of the size of the loan. This is almost a contradiction of the statement that emphasis is placed on the borrower rather than the collateral. An explanation, however, suggests itself. This practice keeps the farmer from spreading his indebtedness among various agencies and thereby facilitates a single and thus more workable repayment schedule. Again, the conditional sales contract by its nature covers only the item or items sold. It is therefore not adaptable to encumbering the additional property owned by the debtor.

A third device in use is the milk check assignment. It is used extensively in all parts of Wisconsin and by all types of agencies. Under this arrangement the borrower or purchaser agrees to pay the indebtedness in fixed amounts out of each milk check. To secure the promise he transfers all right and title to a portion of that check to the lender, who then collects this amount as it becomes due. The borrower thus never sees this money. Out of each check the dairy gives a fixed portion to the lender and the balance of the check to the farmer. To make the assignment a valid legal document it is necessary for the dairy and the farmer to have a contract for the delivery and purchase of milk. The assignment usually incorporates this contract, as we shall subsequently note.

Because of the rule against mortgaging property which is to be acquired, another device in use is the power of attorney. A power of attorney generally is a device whereby an individual grants another authority or power to do certain acts in his name. Although the borrower cannot give a valid mortgage on property which is not yet owned, he can give a power of attorney to a party named by the lender, and the document authorizes this third party to execute the mortgage when the property does come into existence or is acquired by the borrower.

Another device designed to hurdle the after-acquired property problem is the bank draft which incorporates a bill of sale. The draft is given by the lender to the borrower in a fixed or indefinite amount to enable him to purchase certain property. When the purchase is made, the property acquired is described on the face of the draft. The draft is given to the seller in payment. By the act of cashing the draft the seller executes a bill of sale of the property. This runs to the lender, and the lender by virtue of the bill of sale acquires title to the property as security for the indebtedness. Meanwhile the purchaser or borrower has taken possession of the goods. The seller gets his sale price by cashing the draft, the borrower gets the chattel, and the lender gets legal title to the goods to secure the loan which was made. Were it not for the after-acquired rule the lender would, of course, give the money directly to the borrower and immediately take back a mortgage on the goods which the borrower contemplates buying with the money loaned. As it is, a mortgage eventually replaces the bill of sale used in the initial transaction.

Other less popular devices in use are the reservation of title to crops by a landlord as security for rent payments, the assignment of insurance policies, and the pledge of United States government bonds. Of these three, the pledge agreement warrants a definition. In return for a loan of money, the borrower actually delivers possession of property owned by him to the lender. The lender holds the property until the loan is repaid. If it is not repaid the lender by following statutory procedure can sell the goods and apply the proceeds to the loan. Possession in the lender is a requisite of the device.

The pledge agreement is perhaps the oldest and simplest form of security arrangement. Each of the other devices involve safeguards necessitated by a departure from the basic notion of the pledge. Thus, where possession is given to the debtor, as in the conditional sale or the mortgage, public recordation of the security right replaces the transfer of possession which would accompany the pledge. Limitations on the right of the debtor to sell or dispose of the asset are necessary when possession remains in the debtor. The problem never arises when possession is transferred.

An introduction to the pledge would be incomplete without the observation that it is generally unsuited for many farm loan transactions. Possession of the dairy herd and machinery obviously cannot be transferred if the farm operation is to continue. It can, of course, be used where the security is a cash crop. But even here storage facilities maintained by the average credit institution are not suitable.

3. THE PROPOSED UNIFORM COMMERCIAL CODE

As has been noted, there has been relatively little legislation which has altered in any way the substance of the court-made rules covering chattel secured transactions. However, the proposed Uniform Commercial Code, attempting as it does a codification of the commercial law of the entire nation, proposes changes in substance as well as changes in procedure. The Code, the work of legal scholars, is indeed bold innovation, and it fills a vacuum between law and practice that could not be filled by the relative ineffectiveness of sporadic legislation.

When the final draft of the proposed code was submitted in the Spring of 1950, it must have struck many interested parties that here, finally, was proposed legislation which represented the combined thinking of eminent lawyers, professors of law, and judges and which attempted to make needed changes in the substance of law. The proposed legislation was broad and sweeping in its nature; existing acts regulating commercial transactions were to be repealed and this one uniform act was to replace them. The proposed code was founded on the concept of "commercial transactions" as a single, interrelating field susceptible to control by a single act.

The drafting of the Code was done by members of the faculties of leading law schools, and discussion and comment was solicited from judges, lawyers, and professors of law. Finally, the Code was examined and debated by the American Law Institute and the National Conference of Commissioners on Uniform State Laws.[10]

Of particular interest to this study is Article 9 of the Code—"Secured Transactions." This article proposes that we no longer think in terms of the chattel mortgage, the conditional sale, and the various other devices discussed above. It proposes, rather, that we recognize that they are all devices to secure repayment of a loan or the payment of a purchase price and therefore should be called security interests and treated alike, except insofar as the nature of the security itself demands individual treatment. Article 9 of the Code thus replaces form with function, and that in itself is a bold and desirable step. It goes even farther by doing away with the objections to a security right in property which is to be acquired, by establishing a power of sale and disposition of encumbered assets in the borrower, and by adopting a commercial standard for foreclosure sales.

Obviously, therefore, any discussion of chattel secured farm credit must take into account the provisions of the proposed code. The following chapters discuss the prevailing commercial practices in farm credit, the relation of these practices to existing law, and, finally, the relation of these practices to the proposed Uniform Commercial Code.[11]

CHAPTER TWO

Making the loan

1. SECURITY IN CROPS

Practices in the creation of the crop mortgage

The crop mortgage is not used extensively in financing Wisconsin agriculture. It has, however, attained some prominence in tobacco production, in potato production, and some instances of its use also appear in financing dairying. In the tobacco and potato areas, the crop often serves as sole security for the loan. However, its appearance as security in dairy production is attributable to the fact that some credit institutions require a first lien on all of the farmer's personal property, including crops. In this all-inclusive mortgage, little reliance is placed on the crop for security as such. The loaning agency contemplates the harvest of the crop and its use as feed for the livestock covered by the mortgage. By including crops and feed in the mortgage, the mortgagee, if he must take possession of the livestock, is in a position to take possession of feed for them. He also deters the farmer from converting the crops and food supply into cash, thereby in part assuring care of the livestock. Finally, he is in a position to prevent unsecured creditors from levying on this food supply.[1]

The crops covered by the mortgage are described by reference to the real estate on which they are grown. If the crop has been harvested, the real estate on which the drying shed or warehouse is located is described.

The provision for security in crops is generally limited to crops which are growing or harvested and often appears as a part of the printed form.[2] There are instances, however, of the mortgage being taken before the crops are planted. Certain practices have developed to meet this contingency. One such practice, in use in Vernon County, for example, is to have the farmer execute a mortgage on the crops at the time that the loan is made and then date it and file it after the crop is growing. Another is to have the farmer simply execute a mortgage on all crops growing or to be grown during the term of the mortgage. Both of these are isolated instances.

A more popular device in use throughout the state is to have the farmer execute a promise to execute and deliver a mortgage on all crops when they become growing crops.[3] This promise may be accompanied by a power of attorney in someone designated by the bank authorizing the execution and delivery of the mortgage in the event that the debtor fails or refuses to do so.[4] The power is declared irrevocable. This notion is expanded in the Northern potato area in a provision in some forms by which the borrower holds the crop in trust for the mortgagee. Such forms provide that the trust will terminate when a mortgage is executed. Further, the land on which the crop is to be grown is leased and the possession thereof surrendered to the mortgagee until such time as a mortgage on the growing crop is executed. If the mortgagor remains in possession—which he always does—he does so as agent of the lessee-mortgagee.[5]

Practices seek to circumvent the Wisconsin rule

These various methods of attempting to encumber unplanted crops illustrate a conflict between judicial rules and the desires of business men regulated by those rules. Accordingly, the business men with the aid of their attorneys have developed forms, mortgage clauses, and new legal devices to accomplish an end which the court has prohibited. The banker who makes a production loan to the tobacco farmer or the potato farmer desires and needs a secured interest in the crop to be grown; yet at the time the loan is made the crop is not in existence. Similarly, the banker who loans money to the dairy farmer may want a security interest in an unplanted crop which, when harvested, will be used to feed the dairy cattle covered by his mortgage.

The Wisconsin court, however, unlike most other jurisdictions, has never recognized the validity of a mortgage on after-acquired property. The rule as applied to crops invalidates a mortgage which is executed and delivered prior to the time that the crops become growing crops.[6] The purported mortgage, if it includes language giving the mortgagee a right of entry, does give the holder authority to enter upon the land and take possession of the crop after it acquires existence. However, this authority or license may be revoked by the grantor at any time prior to the time that the mortgagee takes possession of the crop. It is not, then, a transfer of any rights in the crop; whatever security the creditor gets can be defeated by the debtor at the last instant.[7]

In terms of the practices discussed above, it seems clear that the first two devices mentioned give the lender little in the way of security. The mortgage given before the crops are grown transfers no right to the crop either presently or in the future. If the mortgage language includes a right to enter upon the land where the crop is growing, the holder of this mortgage could invoke this right to take possession of the crop. But, as has been noted, this license to enter and take possession can be revoked at any time prior to the mortgagee's entry. If the license were considered irrevocable, the mortgage given before the crops are planted would create a valuable right in the mortgagee. But the court has declared that this license can be revoked by the mortgagor.[8]

The practice of postdating and postfiling the mortgage has value only insofar as it besets the mortgagor with the problem of proving that the mortgage was in fact given before the crops were grown. If he can establish this, the mortgagee would then have acquired no right to the crop. The practice might also deter subsequent creditors from levying on the crop or purchasers from buying the crop. That is, the written record would show it as a valid mortgage, and subsequent creditors or purchasers might not ascertain that it was in fact invalid.

Although it is not possible summarily to dismiss the other practices noted, their success in creating a security interest in the crop is dubious. To sustain the promise to execute a mortgage when the crop comes into existence as creating a security interest in the crop, the court would have to adopt the theory that since a court of equity would enforce the promise, the promise itself creates an equitable lien on the crop from the time that it comes into existence. It is clear, however, that a present grant of goods to be acquired cannot in itself be sustained as an equitable lien. This position was argued and rejected in the Chynoweth case.[9] But suppose that instead of a present grant you have a written promise to execute a mortgage. The court was urged in *Hunter* v. *Bosworth* [10] to reverse the Chynoweth decision on the ground that the English courts had since adopted the equitable lien theory.[11] This the court refused to do. But on page 591 of the opinion, the court did recognize a possible distinction between a present grant of goods to be acquired and an express promise to execute a subsequent mortgage. The court said:

> Whether, and in what cases, chattel mortgages containing express covenants for further mortgages to cover after-acquired goods, could be specifically enforced, where there are no intervening adverse rights, after the goods have been acquired, is a question we need not answer here.

This statement of the court suggests the possibility of some rights between the parties greater than the revocable license as defined in the Chynoweth case. There is no discoverable elaboration of this possibility in the cases decided since *Hunter* v. *Bosworth*. The court, however, has since reaffirmed the revocable license theory in controversies between the parties.[12] There is, therefore, no reason to believe that a promise to execute a mortgage will create any security rights as against third parties; there is very little hope that it will do more as between the parties themselves.

If the promise to execute the mortgage when the crop comes into existence does not create any security in the crop, is the creditor in a better position by reason of his power of attorney to execute and deliver the mortgage? The power of attorney by its terms [13] comes into operation after the debtor refuses to execute and deliver the mortgage promised. The act of refusal to execute the mortgage would imply an attempted revocation of the power. The problem then is whether the power created by the document is irrevocable, as it is stated to be.

There are cases in other jurisdictions which hold that a power of attorney given for purposes of securing a debt due the holder is irrevocable. These cases seem to proceed on the theory that the instrument itself creates a lien on the property and that a court of equity will give effect to the intention of the parties.[14] The Wisconsin court could not consistently adopt this reasoning since it has already rejected the equitable lien as supporting security rights in after-acquired property and has declared a right of entry in the mortgagee a revocable license. It would apparently have no difficulty in rejecting the line of authority which upholds the power of attorney as irrevocable.

The power of attorney, the lease provisions, and the trust provisions are all deliberate attempts on the part of the draftsman of these forms to accomplish by indirect means what cannot be accomplished directly, namely, security for the lender in crops which are to be grown. It is not likely that the court will permit form to triumph over substance. The case of *Lamson* v. *Moffat* is directly in point.[15] Murphy, the owner of a farm, entered into a lease agreement with Lamson by which possession of the farm was purportedly surrendered to Lamson and by which Murphy was to do all the work on the farm and live in the dwelling house. The lease agreement was executed before any crops were planted. After the crops were growing, Murphy gave a mortgage on the crop to Moffat. Moffat thus claimed the crops as mortgagee while Lamson claimed them as a tenant of Murphy and therefore owner of the crops. The court held that it was competent to show that the lease was intended to secure Lamson for a claim against Murphy, regardless of its form, and that if the lease was in fact intended as security it was to be treated as a mortgage and therefore void because the property was not in existence when the lease was given. If we apply the theory of *Lamson* v. *Moffat* to the forms under discussion, they appear to be ineffectual in creating security rights. The intention of having a mortgage is expressed clearly. Thus the power of attorney comes into operation if the debtor refuses to execute the *mortgage;* the lease is to be terminated when the *mortgage* is executed; the *lender* is the beneficiary of the trust; the trustee need not account to the debtor if he executes a *mortgage* to the lender.[16] Further, one of the forms refers to a *loan* as consideration,[17] another speaks of *securing* the payment of [X] dollars.[18]

Since the purpose of the forms and practices is a security right in unplanted crops, a right which cannot be accomplished by direct means, and since the court has stated that form will not triumph over substance,[19] it is reasonable to conclude that the forms would not accomplish their purpose if put to a court test. Having said that, however, we must also recognize that they are not only in use but, from the standpoint of farm credit, successfully so. The fact that they are used successfully cannot be scientifically explained; that is, it cannot be accurately stated that lenders use them because they believe that the law would give them their intended effect, or that knowing that the forms have no validity, they nonetheless feel that an uninformed debtor will abide by the written word. Apparently both situations exist. For example, one form of the power of attorney is used extensively by the Production Credit associations. A well-founded assumption seems to be that the form was drafted by attorneys for the United States Department of Agriculture who were very much aware of the problem. The form was doubtless drafted under the assumption that a strong argument could be made for its validity in the states where mortgages on unplanted crops are not permitted. In another situation, an attorney who drafted a similar power of attorney for a finance company stated that he didn't know how effective it would be in a court test but that it would be effective in getting the debtors to execute the mortgage upon demand. It seems clear that the people who use these forms, the lenders and borrowers who are not legally trained, place a great deal of emphasis on the written word. In most situations whatever the form says is considered the "law" on that subject.

Effect of the proposed Code on the creation of crop mortgages

Article 9 of the Uniform Commercial Code is designed to channel thinking in the field of chattel secured transactions away from the device used and into thinking in terms of the function which the security agreement is to serve. It does this by having the article apply to any transaction intended to have effect as security in personal property,[20] by its classification of goods,[21] and by its distinctions based on the class of goods involved.

Thus a security interest in crops is contemplated by the Code. So far as production credit is concerned, crops are classified as "farm products." [22] A security interest in future crops can be accomplished by an after-acquired clause, but such clause will not affect crops which are planted more than [X] years after the agreement is executed. Each state legislature may thus determine its own policy on how many future crops its farmers may encumber. When the security interest in crops is given in connection with a real estate transaction, that is, a lease, a land contract, or a land purchase mortgage, it will attach to all crops grown during the term of the real estate transaction.[23] The security agreement and the financing statement must contain a description of the land on which the crop is growing or to be grown.[24]

The adoption of the Code will then permit a production loan secured in part by crops to be grown, a practice which now exists only through the use of makeshift devices, all of which are of doubtful validity. Present methods of description will not be changed by the Code.

2. SECURITY IN LIVESTOCK

Practices in the creation of the livestock mortgage

Every credit institution visited in the course of this study indicated that the dairy herd is preferred to all other types of farm chattel property offered as security. Depreciation of the dairy herd proceeds at a slower pace than other types of farm personalty, the resale value is less likely to vary during the term of the loan, and it is the primary source of income in the Wisconsin farm economy.

Considerable variance was found in the methods of describing dairy cattle. Breed or color and location are used uniformly. Beyond this it is not possible to generalize. Some banks and their attorneys prefer ear tag numbers when the cattle have been tested and tagged; others object to this practice because of the danger of loss of the tag. One attorney visited took the extreme caution of making a trip to the farm to tattoo the ears of each cow covered.

Some agencies designate the particular number of cattle covered by the mortgage; others prefer to use the word "all" in designating the number. Approximate age may be stated, or the breakdown may be in terms of milk cows, heifers, and calves.

The mortgage forms used by the agencies visited specifically provided that the mortgage was intended to cover the increase of the livestock mortgaged. The clauses as worded make no distinction between increase presently conceived and future increase. They are intended to cover both.[25] Only in one form was a distinction made between male increase and female increase.[26]

The variations in descriptive practices noted in relation to describing dairy cattle appear again in describing beef cattle and hogs. Location is very important, as is breed or color. Ear tags are not used, and greater reliance is placed on descriptive markings.

Existing law—its relation to practices in creating livestock mortgages

The practice of not designating a specified number of cattle in the mortgage is supported by the lender on two grounds: (1) if the farmer purchases additional cattle of the same breed the mortgage will on its face cover these cattle, and (2) if at the time of the mortgage, the farmer has more cattle than the mortgage states and those which are to be covered are not specifically described the mortgage may be void for uncertainty.

The latter proposition is supported by case law.[27] For example, if the mortgage says "25 Holstein cattle, ages 3 to 10, located on my farm in Beaver Township" and the farmer in fact has 26 cattle of that age, the courts take the position that the cattle to be covered are not ascertained and the mortgage is void. This pitfall can be avoided by the use of the word "all." It may be difficult to prove which ones the farmer owned at the time of the mortgage, but the mortgage is otherwise valid.[28] The pitfall noted above may also be avoided by making a complete inventory of the personal property at the time the loan is made, but this is difficult to do if a large herd of beef cattle or a large number of hogs is involved.

The possibility of covering cattle acquired after the execution of the mortgage by the use of the word "all," as is suggested by the first proposition above, is successful only so far as a contesting party is beset with difficulties as to proof of what cattle were owned at the time the mortgage was executed. However, the difficulty of proof might well deter other purchasers or creditors from contesting the mortgagee's claim.

The effect of court decisions on business practices is shown by the clause covering increase. *Funk v. Paul* [29] held that a mortgage given on a cow during the gestation period covered the increase even though the mortgage did not specifically so provide. As against a subsequent purchaser or mortgagee, however, the lien on the increase is invalid after the young is separated from the mother. The precedent for the practice of specifically including the increase in the mortgage document was set by the court when it suggested that the results of the case would have been otherwise if the content of the mortgage document had been such as to give a subsequent purchaser or mortgagee of the calf actual or constructive notice of prior rights in the calf.[30]

The question of whether the specific provision in the forms [31] for all increase covers increase not yet conceived at the time the mortgage is given remains unanswered. This is a very complicated subject, and a variety of holdings can be reached and reconciled. For example, increase not conceived and therefore not in being at the time the mortgage is executed may be considered after-acquired property. As such, the mortgage would not attach. On the other hand, the court could conclude that the chattel mortgage passes legal title to the mother, and in law the owner of the mother owns the offspring.[32] Further, the possible holdings could be affected by whether or not the mortgage specifically mentions increase. Finally, it is customary in dairy farming for the farmer to sell all male increase and keep the better female increase. Because the custom exists and the lender is aware of it, can a mortgage covering increase be said to intend the inclusion of male increase?

Assume that the mortgage covers increase, as the forms in use do. This may mean (1) it covers all increase, male or female, which are conceived and not conceived; (2) it covers all increase, male or female, which are conceived at the time the mortgage is executed; (3) it covers all female increase conceived or not conceived; or (4) it covers all female increase conceived only. Now assume that the mortgage does not mention increase. As has been noted above, *Funk* v. *Paul* said that a mortgage on a cow given during the gestation period covers increase whether mentioned or not. Since in Wisconsin legal title passes by the mortgage, will this mortgage also cover those not conceived? Will it cover male increase, or will the prevailing custom change this? In those states which adopt the theory that a chattel mortgage passes equitable title, increase must be specifically mentioned.[33] It is apparent that a variety of holdings are possible by shifting emphasis between gestation period, specific mention of the increase, and the legal or equitable theory of a chattel mortgage.

These various possibilities have been discussed only in the interest of demonstrating the ramifications of the increase problem. From a law in action viewpoint, it seems clear that few lenders can possibly be aware of the various complications which may arise from any provision relating to increase. In practice, however, the provision is there; it purportedly covers all increase and thus has the desired psychological effect. Also from a law in action viewpoint, it is clear that these various holdings have no functional value. The lender is not really concerned about the sale of male increase, about gestation, and about legal title. He is concerned with having a security interest in the dairy herd as such and in the income produced therefrom. To the extent that increase becomes a part of this dairy herd, he wants his mortgage to cover it.

Effect of the proposed Code on creation of livestock mortgages

It does not appear that the Code will alter existing methods of describing livestock. The descriptions used vary in accordance with what the draftsman thinks will best identify the cattle. The Code requirement is that the property be reasonably identified by the description.[34] The question of using a specific number or the word "all" will still be with us, but the Code's approval of an interest in after-acquired property will alleviate the problem. We can anticipate that most security documents affecting livestock will include after-acquired provisions. The credit agency, whether it uses a definite number or the word "all," intends to cover the entire dairy herd, and the agency would like, if possible, to cover those to be acquired by birth, purchase, or any other method.

The problem of providing for a security interest in the increase of livestock under the Code is not insoluble, but there are traps for the unwary. To restate the problem in issue, we are concerned with whether the security document must mention increase specifically and whether the increase covered includes that not yet conceived as well as that which is conceived.

No clear-cut answer is given to the first question, but an examination of the Code indicates that increase will not be covered unless the document specifically so provides. Section 9-204 provides that a security interest cannot attach until an agreement is made that it attach. Weight is added to this argument by Section 9-202, which provides that title to the collateral is immaterial. It will be recalled that the basis for saying that a mortgage attaches to the increase though no mention is made thereof is the theory that the mortgagee has legal title to the mother.

If under the Code there must be specific mention of the increase, what increase can be covered? and how is this accomplished? The Code approves an interest in after-acquired property, as we have noted. Since no time limit is placed on future increase, it is clear that all increase during the life of the security interest can be covered if the lender desires.[35] However, a security interest in the cow plus an after-acquired clause will not of itself take care of all increase. Section 9-204(2)(a) provides that the debtor has no right in the young of livestock until they are conceived. Conversely, then, the debtor's rights attach at the time of conception. Since the debtor has a present interest in that increase which is conceived, the lender cannot claim it under an after-acquired clause. After-acquired property by definition in the Code will not include property in which the debtor has a present interest. If my interpretation of Section 9-204 is correct, specific mention must be made of increase for it to be covered, and according to the foregoing analysis, security interest in the cow alone does not include increase already conceived. It follows that the security agreement to be complete must provide for an interest in the cow, an interest in increase presently conceived—both of which will attach at the time of the agreement by Section 9-204(1)—and an after-acquired clause for increase not yet conceived. This careful drafting will be particularly important for purchase-money lenders. Section 9-312(4) provides that a purchase-money security interest is prior to a conflicting interest in the same collateral claimed under an after-acquired property clause. Since conception increases the value of the cow, the purchase-money lender should have security in everything he is loaning money for. Yet if no provision is made by him for increase conceived, the purchase-money lender stands to lose security which should be his.

3. Security in equipment

Practices

The farmer's machinery is included in the usual farm mortgage. It is described by the type of machine, the brand name, and by model. In some instances the serial number is added, particularly on new equipment. Thus the description will be something like this: "One John Deere corn planter, Model 91, Ser. 12345." Generally, no specific provision is made for covering trade-ins, replacements, or after-acquired machinery except to the extent that an all-inclusive after-acquired clause appears.[36] The problem of trade-ins and replacements raises, of course, the twin problems of authority to sell and of security in after-acquired property. The two problems arise in dealing with all types of farm chattel property used for security.

There are objections on the part of many lenders, particularly the banking institutions, to security in machinery alone. Apparently at times there is no ready market for used machinery, and the rate of depreciation is very rapid.

The unwillingness on the part of bankers to limit their security to machinery accounts in part for the greater importance of the chattel mortgage over the conditional sale contract even in financing machinery purchases. As an accommodation, however, some banks do purchase conditional sale paper from local machinery dealers.[37] The finance companies are considerably more active in this field. Both types of institutions purchase this paper on recourse agreement. The recourse agreement may take one of two forms. It may be an agreement whereby the lender in the event of buyer's default reassigns the contract to the dealer for the balance due on the contract. The dealer must then proceed against the buyer. The other form provides that the dealer is not obligated for the balance due after default until such time as the lending agency repossesses the property and returns it to the dealer.

The Production Credit associations have developed a novel procedure in financing the purchase of chattels. It is used particularly in financing purchase of farm equipment, though it is not necessarily so limited. Suppose the farmer wishes to purchase a new tractor and needs money to finance it. He does not know when or where he will buy it but wants to be in a position to do so when the occasion arises. The Production Credit association could advance the money and take a mortgage on any tractor thereafter owned, but this would be invalid under the after-acquired rule. Until the tractor was purchased the association would not be secured. The method followed is to give the farmer a bank draft which incorporates a bill of sale.[38] The draft is given by the farmer to the dealer, and the dealer executes the bill of sale to the Production Credit association. Thus the draft is honored only for the purchase of the specific item. When the farmer executes a mortgage on the tractor to the association the title acquired under the bill of sale is relinquished and replaced by title under the mortgage.

Law and Code provisions affecting equipment purchase

The legal questions posed by a discussion of methods used to finance equipment purchases are (1) the respective advantages of the chattel mortgage and the conditional sales contract, and (2) the validity of the bill of sale as presently used. These questions are basic in certain aspects of farm credit and will be discussed in detail in the succeeding chapters on protection against third parties and remedies against default on security. For the time being it is appropriate to discuss here briefly the provisions in the proposed Uniform Commercial Code affecting equipment purchases.

The principal effect of the Code on farm machinery financing, in terms of existing practices, is the abolition of the distinction between a chattel mortgage and a conditional sale.[39] The bill of sale bank draft form used by the Production Credit association is made unnecessary by the after-acquired provisions of the Code and by also the Code's recognition that a purchase-money security interest can exist in a third party lender as well as a seller.[40] This does not suggest that the forms will not be used. It does mean that a security interest is created by the form and as such it will be regulated by the Code.[41]

4. Milk check assignments

The chattel mortgage or conditional sales contract when used to secure a loan to a dairy farmer is usually accompanied by an assignment to the lender of a percentage of the proceeds of the dairy products to be sold. The device usually serves as a convenient method for amortizing the loan. In only a few instances does the assignment serve as the only security for the loan.

The forms used to accomplish the assignment are many and varied, but they fall into four general groups. The simplest form consists of an order signed by the farmer-debtor which directs the creamery with which he does business to deliver a percentage or a fixed amount of each of the farmer's checks to the credit agency until the loan is paid.[42]

The second group of forms includes the order set forth in the simple form and a provision whereby the creamery accepts the provisions of the assignment.[43] Some, but not all, of the forms in this group have a clause according to which the farmer agrees to deliver his milk to the named creamery until the loan is paid in full.[44]

The third group improves upon the second by always including an agreement by the farmer to deliver his milk to the named creamery until the debt is paid and an agreement by the creamery to purchase the debtor's milk as a part of its acceptance of the assignment.[45]

The fourth group incorporates a three-way agreement whereby the farmer agrees to sell his milk to the named creamery and authorizes a delivery of a percentage of the proceeds to the lender and the creamery agrees to buy the milk at prevailing prices and deliver the agreed percentage of the proceeds to the lender.[46]

Legal effect of milk check assignments

Although the simple order directing the creamery to pay a percentage of funds to the lender serves as a convenient repayment plan, it does not create any legal rights. The Wisconsin court has refused to recognize the validity of a partial assignment unless the obligor, in this case the creamery, assents thereto.[47] Although the lender may surmount this difficulty by having the order accepted by the creamery, another line of cases hold that no security rights are created in the absence of a valid contract giving existence to the fund assigned.[48]

This position is an extension of the rule against transferring property to be acquired. In the usual case in which the dairy farmer delivers his milk daily to the creamery without any contract, the assignment gives no claim to the proceeds of future milk deliveries. It may be revoked by the debtor at any time prior to the collection of the money by the lender. This, then, is similar to the revocable license theory discussed previously.[49] There is no priority against garnishing creditors. Nevertheless, in spite of its legal weakness, the economic convenience of the milk check assignment has given the device widespread popularity.

If there is a valid contract between the creamery and the farmer for delivery the contract creates a present right in the proceeds of future deliveries. It is then no longer a right to be acquired, and a valid assignment can be made of all payments to become due.[50] The forms which include a contract between the creamery and the farmer are thus designed to meet the requirements for a valid assignment.

Effect of the Code on the milk check assignment

If a valid contract exists between the creamery and the farmer, a contract right exists which can be the subject of a security interest under the Code.[51] If, as in the usual case, there is only a habit of daily delivery, the farmer has an account,[52] and that is also properly subject to a security interest. By use of an after-acquired clause, future milk accounts can be covered by the security agreement.[53]

5. Marketing contracts

Coöperative marketing associations enter into long term contracts with their farmer members by which the farmer agrees to deliver his crop to the association for orderly marketing. Private canning companies enter into similar contracts and may also furnish special seed to the farmer under the contract. Many state statutes provide that the coöperative shall be entitled to specific performance of its contract.[54] However, the right of the canning company to specific performance is not always clear.[55]

The canner accordingly is interested in a property right in the crop not only to assure delivery of the crop but to secure the advance of seed as well. The crop mortgage arrangement is not available because the contract is executed and the seed necessarily advanced before the planting season. Various devices are used by the canning company. By one device the canning company leases the land from the farmer and makes him an employee for the planting and harvesting of the crop. By another device the canner enters into a bailment contract with the farmer by which title to the seed and the product remains in the canner. Both devices would probably be declared invalid chattel mortgages as an obvious attempt to circumvent state policy.

Under the proposed Uniform Commercial Code the problem presented is capable of solution. If the coöperative or canning company advances seed or other financial aid it can provide for a security interest in the crop to secure the contractual obligation of the farmer to deliver. A security interest is defined as an interest in property which secures the performance of an obligation as well as the payment of money.[56] If there is just a straight contract for delivery and no agreement for a security interest, the contracting purchaser may still be able to protect his interest in the crop under a provision in Article 2 on Sales.[57]

6. Pledge agreements [58]

No instances were found in which the farmer pledged tangible chattel property as security. There were instances, however, in which instruments evidencing a right to money, such as insurance policies or United States government bonds, were accepted by and delivered to the bank as collateral. Agreements setting forth the terms of the delivery were a part of the transaction.[59]

Field-warehousing, the well-known hybrid of pledge transactions, is apparently not used in financing the farmer directly. At least the practice was not discovered.[60] Field-warehousing practices do, however, indirectly affect Wisconsin agriculture insofar as they are used to finance canning companies that purchase farm crops. By virtue of an agreement between the canning company, the bank, and the warehouse company, the canner delivers canned goods to an agent of the warehouse company. This agent, who is also an employee of the canner, issues a receiving report. This report is then delivered to the bank, which in reliance thereon advances credit to the canner measured by an agreed amount per case delivered.

When the canning company wishes to sell any of the goods so pledged a release is prepared by the warehouse company. This release together with the canner's check in partial repayment of the loan is delivered to the bank. The bank by signing the release authorizes the warehouse company to deliver the designated number of cases to the canner. A continuing financing arrangement is thus put in motion whereby money is advanced as needed and payments are accepted as they can be made.

The fiction of the entire field-warehousing arrangement is evidenced by the fact that the goods are actually stored on the premises of the canner and by the further fact that an employee of the canner acts as the agent of the warehouse company in arranging the details of storing and releasing. The device is nonetheless intended and used to satisfy the change of possession requirements of the pledge transaction. Instead of the bank actually receiving possession in its place of storage, the warehouse company acts for the bank and goes to the canner's place of business to take possession. The use of the canner's employee in the dual role further facilitates the workability of the device, even as it adds to the fiction.

The proposed Uniform Commercial Code, apparently in recognition of the fiction, requires, as we shall note later, that notice be given of the arrangement by public record. It is clear that the Code does not consider storage on the premises adequate notice of the security right, even though change of possession is normally adequate notice to third parties. The Code's recognition of the inventory lien and its accompanying freedom of disposition in the lender will also make the field-warehousing device lose much of its attraction under present law.

7. LANDLORD-TENANT SECURITY ARRANGEMENTS

Practices in creating security rights in landlords

In those few areas of Wisconsin where farm tenancy is common, instances were discovered in which landlords secure rent payments by security provisions inserted in the lease. The security interest may be incorporated in the lease agreement and may require the tenant to give a chattel mortgage on all crops to the landlord.[61] A more usual provision is one whereby the landlord reserves title to the crops grown during the term of the lease. In the absence of such a provision title to the crops is in the tenant.

Another method used to protect landlords is the so-called cropper's contract. Its use is particularly prominent in the tobacco areas of the state. Under this contract lease provisions are avoided; instead, an employer-employee relationship is established between the owner and the operator of the farm. The cropper contract in essence is a device to keep ownership of the crop in the owner of the farm. To rebut the presumption that a lease is created, care is used to make the operator a "cropper" as far as the dairy herd or other personalty are concerned.

The usual lease agreement has no security provisions. It usually provides either by oral or simple written agreement for a "fifty-fifty" arrangement. The landlord and tenant are each treated as owning an undivided one-half interest in the farm personalty. When a tenant under such an agreement is financed by a credit institution, a mortgage on his undivided one-half interest is taken by the lender. Because there may be particular arrangements between the landlord and tenant as to ownership of certain items [62] some agencies require that the landlord agree in writing that his interest in the property is an undivided one-half and that a division will be made in the event that the tenant defaults on the mortgage.[63]

Legal effect of lease-security provisions

The practices and results of the practices become clear when we recall that a lease is a conveyance of an estate in land from the landlord to the tenant. As the owner of the possessory interest the tenant owns the crops grown during the term of the lease. As the owner of the crops the tenant has a right to give a valid chattel mortgage. However, under the Wisconsin rule he can mortgage only those which are in existence. Thus the mortgage provisions of the lease are valid only as to the crops which are growing when the lease is executed.[64]

Although one of the normal attributes of a possessory interest is ownership of the crops, the landlord, the owner of the nonpossessory interest, may in conveying the possessory interest withhold certain of the possessory rights. One such reservation may be title to the crops grown during the term of the lease. Thus the practice of reserving title in the landlord affects not only the growing crops but all crops planted during the term. This security provision is not invalidated by the rule against after-acquired property.[65] The reservation of title, then, is effective security; the mortgage is not.[66]

The owner of land may also hire an individual to operate his farm and withhold all normal possessory rights. He may pay this individual in money or goods, and the goods may be part or all of the crops grown. So long as he avoids words which create a possessory estate in land, the individual hired remains a "cropper" and does not get title to the crops or receive other possessory rights.[67] Evidence of the creation of a cropper contract rather than a lease is that the capital and expense outlay is provided entirely by the owner of the land and all rights of management are reserved in the owner of the land. If a cropper contract does exist, the owner of the land is the owner of the crop, and the cropper cannot give a valid mortgage. This last statement suggests another reason why some private institutions require an ownership agreement signed by the landlord.

It is interesting to observe at this point that the courts have been willing to uphold security rights in unplanted crops as far as landlords are concerned but have not done so where lenders are concerned. They have done this by a reliance on theories of real property law—that is, on the theory that the owner of land may grant all or a portion of his estate. It is not then a matter of the tenant granting an interest in the crop; instead, it is a matter of the landlord never having surrendered rights to the crop. Thus the maxim "a man cannot grant or charge that which he hath not" does not arise to plague us. In terms of function, however, there is no apparent reason in the Wisconsin farm economy why a landlord should have security in unplanted crops when the lender cannot.

Effect of the Code on lease agreements

Article 9 of the proposed Commercial Code applies to any transaction which is intended to create a security interest in goods. Goods include growing crops.[68] By use of an after-acquired clause in the agreement, the interest will attach to all crops grown during the term of the lease, even though the term is longer than the prescribed period fixed by the legislature for a security interest in crops not connected with a lease agreement.[69]

Thus, whether the landlord uses a chattel mortgage provision or a title retention provision, the agreement will create an effective security interest in all crops grown during the term of the lease. If he uses the cropper contract it will depend on whether the contract is used or intended to create a security interest. If so, Article 9 will apply. However, it should be recognized that a cropper contract may be desired by the landowner for reasons other than security. As such it will not be affected by the Code.

CHAPTER THREE

Policing and administering secured loans—rights of third parties

The previous chapter discussed the methods used in creating security rights and the extent to which these methods were successful in giving the lender a secured claim against the chattel property of the debtor. Equally important to the lender are the methods by which he may protect his rights in the secured loan and avoid having the interest declared invalid as a result of his own acts. Again, law and practice are at variance in this important area of the chattel secured farm loan transaction.

The majority of lenders file their security documents with the register of deeds in the county in which the property is located.[1] This act of filing is in accordance with a legislative provision and is relied upon to protect the interest of the lender against third parties.[2] But even though they have taken advantage of this initial protection, the subsequent activities of the lender and the debtor raise doubts as to the continued protection afforded the lender. The going ways of commerce are not entirely in harmony with existing requirements, but evidently they are in harmony with the requirements of the proposed Commercial Code.

1. Security in crops

Permission to sell or use the mortgaged crop for feed

After the crop mortgage is executed and filed, the credit agencies generally do not diligently police the crops covered. If the crop is to be used for feed, the farmer is permitted to harvest it, store it, and use it to feed his livestock. If the crop is one produced for cash sale, it is customarily understood between the parties that the farmer is free to negotiate the sale when and with whom he desires without prior consultation with the lender. No effort is made to provide that the mortgage shall attach to the proceeds of the sale. It is true that the mortgage forms specifically deny the existence of any privilege in the farmer to sell the crop without the written consent of the mortgagee.[3] However, it is usual for the farmer to proceed with the sale without this specific written consent; in fact, the provision in the form is unknown to some of those who use it.

In order to protect themselves against possible claims of lenders, tobacco buyers acquire a chattel mortgage abstract prepared from the Register of Deeds chattel mortgage records to ascertain the existence of chattel mortgage liens against crops they propose to buy. Then if a crop is purchased, the buyer makes his check payable to the creditors shown by the abstract. This practice has apparently not yet been established by purchasers of the potato crop.

Legal effect of permission to use or sell the crop

The practices discussed raise legal issues of whether the privileges given the mortgagor of (1) feeding the mortgaged crop or (2) otherwise disposing of it invalidate the mortgage. Insofar as the first question is concerned, the privilege is held valid if the use benefits the mortgagee. Thus in *Knapp, Stout & Co.* v. *Deitz*,[4] the mortgagee had a mortgage on certain supplies which the mortgagor was permitted to use up in the performance of a logging contract. The logging contract was given to the mortgagor by the mortgagee to enable him to reduce the indebtedness. The court held that the use of the supplies was for the benefit of the mortgagee.

In the usual case in which the mortgagee has a mortgage on

crops, other feed, and on the livestock, freedom in the farmer to use mortgaged crops or the mortgaged feed would be valid because such use would be for the benefit of the mortgagee. A clause in some of the forms in use in Wisconsin contemplates just this use of feeds. It provides as follows: "The mortgagor covenants and agrees that the feed stuffs hereby mortgaged, or so much thereof as may be required therefor will be used solely for the purpose of preserving and preparing for market the livestock hereby mortgaged." [5] It is just as clear under Wisconsin law, however, that a privilege in the mortgagor to use up the mortgaged property for his own benefit or in part for his benefit and in part for the benefit of the mortgagee makes the mortgage void and fraudulent as against creditors.[6] The case supporting this rule also involved mortgaged supplies exhausted in logging operations. The logging contract was not let by the mortgagee, however. Although there was a suggestion that the proceeds of the operation would be used to pay the debt, the court felt that the consumption of the security —stock in trade—without direct application to the debt was fraudulent against general creditors.

This holding has a direct application to the usual farm mortgage. If it is certain that all foodstuffs or all crops are used only to care for animals covered by the mortgage, the lender would be protected. Not all farm animals are covered, however—for example, chickens—and even though all animals are covered in the original mortgage, those animals acquired afterwards are free of the mortgage. If the parties are to comply strictly with existing legal doctrine, the farmer-mortgagor would have to maintain separate haystacks and separate granaries and take extreme precaution to see that the mortgaged feed is fed only to the mortgaged livestock. This situation may seem strained, but there is no authority for a less stringent application of the law.

If the crop is one which is usually held for sale, the practice of the mortgagee of permitting the mortgagor complete freedom of disposition amounts to a waiver of the security interest against the buyer of the crop. In Wisconsin this is true against purchasers who do not have actual knowledge of the mortgage. And the fact that the mortgage may be filed does not alter this result as long as the buyer does not actually know of its existence.[7] If the mortgagee permits the mortgagor to sell the property and apply the proceeds to his own use instead of requiring application of the proceeds on the debt, the mortgage has no validity against other creditors of the mortgagor.[8] Thus, in practice if the agreement as to the proceeds is, as usual, undefined, the crop mortgagee may be waiving his security right against creditors as well as against purchasers. Certainly, litigation is encouraged in the usual case. The theory in support of these results is that the lender is substituting the personal promise of the debtor for the security interest, even though this is not the intent of the lender. The lender simply realizes that it is more feasible for the farmer to sell his own crop. The presence of the lender would chill the negotiations. It is suggested, however, that the lender would do well to define more carefully the intent that the proceeds are to be applied on the debt when dealing with mortgages on cash crops.

As has been noted in Chapter II, the proposed Uniform Commercial Code contemplates a security interest in growing crops. By virtue of an after-acquired clause, the agreement will attach to future crops as well as those growing at the time the agreement is executed. The security interest attaches to these future crops when the debtor has rights in the crop—that is, when the crop is planted.[9] The crop secured lender under the Code must file a financing statement or run the risk of having his interest subordinated to purchasers, lien creditors, or subsequent secured lenders who have no knowledge of the prior interest and who perfect their security interest first.[10]

Perfection of the security interest in crops as against lien creditors, purchasers, and subsequent secured lenders by definition occurs when a financing statement [11] is filed, except that if filing occurs before a security interest attaches, the security interest is perfected when the interest attaches.[12] In the case of crops this means that the interest is perfected against such third parties when the crops are planted—assuming, of course, that the statement is filed at that time or prior thereto.

A short history of this provision is necessary to illustrate the difficulties in protecting third party rights. In the Spring, 1950, draft of the Code, Section 9-312(1) stated that an interest attaching after a financing statement is filed took priority from the time of filing. This described the situation in which a loan was made to finance crops to be grown. If the statement was filed at the time of the advance, priority dated from that time, even though the interest in fact attached at a later date—that is, when the crop was planted.

In the September, 1950, revision of Article 9, Section 9-303 (1)(b), relating to perfection of security interests, provided that a security was perfected when the interest attached. In the case of crops this would mean that the interest was perfected when the crops were planted. It was pointed out at the time [13] that this provision taken together with the section then numbered 9-313 might present certain problems, inasmuch as that section provided that when conflicting security interests attach to the same collateral, such interests rank in the order of the time of perfection—not time of filing as in the Spring, 1950, draft. Consequently, two lenders who provided for a security interest in the same future crop would have equal priority. Since both interests would attach at the same moment—when the crop was planted—they would be perfected at the same moment. However, either lender could hurdle this difficulty by virtue of the section then numbered 9-313(2). This section provided that a secured lender who had a perfected security interest and who acquired an interest in after-acquired collateral under the security agreement took priority to such rights in the after-acquired collateral from the time that his interest was originally perfected. A lender who included existing property in his agreement would have priority to the crop from the time his agreement was filed, but the lender who took only the crop to be acquired would have to await the time that the interest attached before his right was perfected. Thus a lender second in time could have priority to the crop if he included existing property and if the first lender did not.

The present draft of the Code, the November, 1951, draft, obviates this problem in part. It will be recalled that the pertinent provision, Section 9-303(1)(a), still provides that perfection occurs when the interest attaches if the statement is on file. However, Section 9-312(1) of this final draft states that an interest which attaches after filing takes priority from the time of filing. This is an exception to the general rule stated in Section 9-312 that conflicting interests rank in the order of time of perfection. Thus when two lenders secure their loan with the same future crop and do not include existing property, priority will go to the one who files first. The problem of possible equal priority created by the September,

1950, revision is to this extent obviated by the reinsertion in part of the Spring, 1950, provision. A problem does remain, however. Section 9-312(1) is expressly subject to 9-312(3), which provides that a secured party who has a perfected security interest—that is, one whose agreement is on file and includes existing property —and who acquires rights in after-acquired collateral under the security agreement takes priority to such rights from the time that his security interest is originally perfected. The following hypothetical case illustrates the problems inherent in these provisions of the proposed code.

Lender A advances money and files a security interest only in the crop to be grown. Subsequently, lender B advances money and files a security interest in a tractor presently owned by the debtor and in the crop to be grown. Neither A nor B is a purchase-money lender. The interest of lender B would be originally perfected before the interest of lender A even though filed later, because B's interest in the tractor would attach before lender A's interest in the crop.

Section 9-312 provides that when conflicting interests attach to the same collateral such interests rank in the order of time of perfection. There are, however, exceptions to this general rule in the subsections which follow. Of interest to us here are the exceptions contained in subsections (1) and (3). Subsection (1) provides that interests which attach after filing take priority from the time of filing. Both A's and B's interest in the crop attaches after filing—specifically, at the moment when the crop becomes growing. By the application of subsection (1) lender A would prevail because of the earlier filing were it not for the fact that subsection (3) provides that a secured party who has a perfected interest and who acquires rights in after-acquired collateral takes priority from the time his security interest was originally perfected. Therefore, lender B would have a protected interest in the tractor earlier than A could possibly have a perfected interest in the crop.

The lenders in this hypothetical case were made nonpurchase-money lenders because subsections (4), (5), and (6) of Section 9-312 of the Code make special provisions for the priorities of purchase-money lenders. We must therefore treat these provisions separately.

Exception (6) is clearly applicable to crops and therefore

establishes the priorities of lenders who make advances to the debtor to enable him to produce the crop. It is not at all clear, however, that exceptions (4) and (5) will be applicable to such lenders. Exceptions (4) and (5) establish the priorities of purchase money security interests as such, and the definition of that phrase in the Code does not seem to include the lender who advances money to enable a debtor to produce a crop. It apparently contemplates only a lender who advances money to enable a debtor to purchase goods already in existence.

Purchase-money security interest is defined in Section 9-107 of the Code as follows:

(a) one taken or retained by the seller of the collateral to secure all or part of its price, or (b) one taken by a person who by making advances or incurring an obligation gives value to enable the debtor to acquire rights in or the use of the collateral if such value is in fact so used, or (c) one taken by a person who for the purpose of enabling the debtor to pay for or acquire rights in or the use of the collateral makes advances or incurs an obligation not more than ten days before or after the debtor receives possession of the collateral even though the value given is not in fact used to pay the price.

Definition (a) might appear to include, for example, the seller of the seed who takes an interest in the crop. It will be noted, however, that the seed is not the collateral. Definition (b) conceivably might include the lender who makes an advance used by the debtor to buy seed. The advance, according to this provision, would enable the debtor to acquire rights in the collateral—in this case the crop. And in definition (c) the language might be construed to include the lender who advances money for seed not more than ten days before or after the debtor plants the crop. But to reach this conclusion the phrase "receives possession" would have to be interpreted to include the act of planting.

The conclusion that the definition of "purchase-money interest" is not intended to apply to the interest of a lender who advances money to enable the debtor to buy seed and takes the crop as security is strengthened by the language of subsection (6) of Section 9-312. This subsection specifically states that when the collateral is crops, the interest of a later secured party who *in order to enable the debtor to produce them* [emphasis mine] makes a new advance, etc. Subsections (4) and (5) both use the phrase "purchase-money security interests," but this phrase does not appear in subsection (6), which relates specifically to crops. The reasonable conclusion is that crops are the subject of separate treatment and not within the purview of subsections (4) and (5).

Subsection (6) has the effect of encouraging the direct production loan in that it declares that a lender who advances money to enable the debtor to produce the crop and takes an interest in the crop as security will be favored over another lender who has an interest in the same crop as security for obligations such as rent, interest, or real estate mortgage principal due more than six months before the crop is planted. To apply under subsection (6), the advance must be made during the production season or not more than three months before the crops are planted. It is noteworthy that exception (6) covers only this instance of conflict between the production lender and the holder of an interest in the crop to secure a real estate obligation.

Exceptions (4) and (5) determine priority between a purchase-money interest and an interest under an after-acquired clause and between two lenders under an after-acquired clause. It seems clear that the situations contemplated by exceptions (4) and (5) are just as likely to arise here to plague the secured lenders who finance the farmer by taking the crop as security as in loan transactions where the collateral is the thing purchased in fact. It may be wise, therefore, to amend or clarify the definition of purchase-money security interest to include an interest taken in the crop when the lender advances money to enable the debtor to produce the crop. If this is done, exceptions (4) and (5) are applicable and the problem is avoided. Because this recommendation is made, and because some courts may interpret the present definitions as including such an enabling loan, an analysis of exceptions (4) and (5) is warranted.

By exception (4) of Section 9-107 a purchase-money security interest has priority over a conflicting interest in the same collateral claimed under an after-acquired clause if the purchase-money interest is perfected at the time the debtor receives the collateral. In our hypothetical case above, if lender A were considered a purchase-money lender—that is, one who specifically makes an advance to enable the debtor to acquire the collateral, for example, a loan to buy the seed for the crop—and lender B were not, A would have priority.[14]

Exception (4) is, however, subject to exception (5), which applies in the case of conflicting purchase-money security interests. Subsection (5) provides that the interest of a seller or of a secured party whose advance *is used* [emphasis mine] at his direction to pay a seller takes priority if he has perfected his interest at the time the debtor receives the collateral or within ten days thereafter. In any other case of conflicting purchase-money interests, lenders rank equally. If both A and B were purchase-money lenders, their priority would be governed by exception (5). If A were a seller of the seed or if A loaned money which was used at his direction to pay the seller of the seed, A would have priority over B, if B's advance, though intended for the purchase of the seed, was in fact used for another purpose. This exception is necessitated by the Code's definition of purchase-money lenders. It will be recalled that the definition includes the seller who takes back a security interest, the secured lender who advances money intended for a purchase price and the money is in fact so used, and the secured lender who advances money within a fixed period intending that it shall be used for a purchase price but which in fact is not.

The lender under the Code who properly files his security interest will be taking the same precautions as the lender who files under existing law. It does not appear, however, that the subsequent practices of the lender under the Code will subject him to the risk that he takes under existing law. If the crop is harvested and used for feed, the interest is not invalidated by reason of such liberty in the farmer. This is true whether the use benefits the secured lender or not.[15] The Code in this respect will clarify any doubts as to the validity of existing practices.

If the crop is one which is to be held for sale, we can at best speculate about the changes that will be effected by the Code. If the secured lender gives his debtor freedom to sell the crop by so providing in his security agreement or otherwise, a buyer will take free of the security interest but the lender will have an interest in any identifiable proceeds.[16] On the other hand, limitations on freedom of disposition are effective against the buyer [17]—that is, the lender's interest continues also in the original collateral.

Some history of the development of the Code is again necessary to clarify a few remaining statements on this subject. Both the Spring, 1950, draft and the September, 1950, revision provided in Section 9-306 that if collateral were sold by the debtor, the security interest would continue in any identifiable proceeds of the debtor. The September, 1950, revision added that "except as otherwise provided in Section 9-307" the security interest continues in the collateral as well. This latter section, Section 9-307(2), provided that in the case of all goods other than inventory (which does not include farm products) limitations on the debtor's authority to sell were effective against a buyer with notice, except that a filed financing statement under which the lender claimed a security interest in proceeds gave the debtor unlimited authority to sell the collateral in the ordinary course of business free of the security interest.

At the time of the September, 1950, revision it seemed reasonable to suppose that practices would not change. It did not appear likely that credit agencies would openly provide in their filed statements for an interest in the proceeds and thereby permit the buyers to take free and clear of the lender's interest. They were more likely to continue the practice of giving the debtor implied authority to sell, because regardless of such authority they would have an interest in the proceeds under Section 9-306 and such implied authority would not affect their interest in the collateral.[18]

A change appearing in the Final Text Edition, November, 1951, requires a re-examination of this position. Section 9-306 [19] now provides that when collateral is sold by the debtor the security interest continues in any identifiable proceeds; and the security interest continues also in the original collateral unless the debtor's action was authorized by the secured party in the security agreement *or otherwise* [emphasis mine]. The insertion of the words "or otherwise" probably means that proof of implied authority to sell by custom or fact will cause the lender to lose his rights in the collateral as against a buyer of the crop.

Will then the lender under the Code openly provide for a lien on the proceeds? He would be well advised to do so. The advantage of leaving it out is gone when the door is opened to proof of implied authority to sell. On the other hand, there are advantages to including an interest in the proceeds in the financing statement. Section 9-306 states, on the question of priority, that the interest in the proceeds is a perfected interest if the interest in the original collateral was perfected but that it ceases to be a perfected interest and becomes unperfected ten days after receipt of the proceeds by the debtor unless (a) the financing statement covering the original collateral *also includes the proceeds* [emphasis mine], or unless (b) it is perfected before the expiration of the ten-day period. By including the proceeds in his statement the lender would not run the risk of failing to file within the ten-day period.

This provision in the Code is not new, but without the provision added in the November, 1951, edition it was doubtful that this advantage of including the proceeds outweighed the advantage of not including them. But because of the change noted above, the advantage of not including them is gone. If under the Code the lender continues to give implied authority to sell, which is the custom now in practice, he would do well to take advantage of the provision for including proceeds in his agreement.

In summary, it seems clear that the lender is in a better position under the Code than he is under existing law. His implied authority to sell will not subject him to a loss of his interest as against creditors.[20] He is in no worse position as against purchasers of the crop. And he is assured of a security interest in the proceeds from the sale of the crop.

2. Security in Livestock

Culling the dairy herd—practice, law, and the Code

Perhaps the most difficult problem for those lenders who finance the operation of the Wisconsin dairy farm is the problem of replacements in the dairy herd. The lender is, of course, principally interested in having the loan repaid. Anything that improves the condition of the dairy herd increases the income of the farmer and in turn increases his ability to repay the loan. Meanwhile, the principal security for the loan is the dairy herd. Some of the cows in that herd may become diseased, they may turn out to be poor producers, or they may, during the term of the loan, reach an age when it is no longer profitable to keep them.

Should the lender permit the farmer to weed out these poorer cattle? From the farmer's viewpoint there is every reason why the answer to this question should be yes. He is certainly in a better position to decide when a poor producer should be removed from the herd, when to emphasize high production at the expense of butter fat content or vice versa, and to decide what increase to keep and what to sell.

The general tendency of the credit institutions seems to be

to give an affirmative answer to this question. But how shall the culling be policed? It is not possible to give a general answer. The methods vary with the individual bankers. The following are some of the answers given by various interviewees.

Some lenders permit the farmer to sell those cattle that he wishes and to use the proceeds as he sees fit. Where the mortgage covers increase, it is very clear that the lender makes no effort to supervise the sale of male increase or the use of the proceeds from such sale. Some lenders are cautious enough to say that the farmer may sell off the cattle as he chooses, provided he makes replacements in the herd. Still other lenders insist that if any cattle are sold, the proceeds of the sale must be applied on the loan. This insistence is made with the understanding that additional money will be advanced for the purchase of replacements. Finally, some lenders require that specific consent be acquired for each sale and that the proceeds be applied on the loan.[21] Even in this rare instance of requiring specific consent, the impression prevails that cattle are sold and replacements made by honest farmers without such prior consent. The farmer reasons that the lender is better off if a poor producer is exchanged for a good one.

We can gather from the attitudes expressed that the lender is not particularly perturbed about the sale of cattle or about the proceeds of those sales. He is, in fact, interested in covering the replacements. The impression is given that if the mortgage could cover replacements in the herd, considerably less emphasis would be placed on the entire problem. A replacement, however, is after-acquired property. Certainly this is true if it is purchased; it may well be true even if it is born of a mortgaged mother. Thus unless the lender insists on a new mortgage for each replacement he is constantly risking a diminution of security. Some lenders accordingly require the execution of a supplemental mortgage on each replacement.[22] Others hesitate to burden good customers with this request. Instead, they make a practice of inspecting the security and drawing a new mortgage each year.

This desire and intention of the lender could be accomplished by a mortgage on the dairy herd as such rather than a mortgage on individual animals, but such a mortgage is not possible under existing law. An analogous situation is the so-called inventory lien common in the financing of business enterprises which have a shifting inventory. Under this arrangement, when new inventory is added to the stock the security interests floats, so-to-speak, so as to cover the new items. Similarly, when goods are sold the burden of the security interest is lifted from those sold. The device was originally subject to the objections noted in the foregoing discussion of prohibition against sale or use of mortgaged property. It is, however, now gaining favor as the only feasible security device for debtors having most of their assets invested in a changing inventory, even though present statutes sanctioning it are often quite stringent as to reports which must be filed.[23]

This shifting lien device with less stringent reporting requirements was sanctioned by the Wisconsin legislature in 1951 in the Factor's Lien Act.[24] This act provides for a continuing lien on merchandise of the borrower whether the property is presently owned and whether or not it is in existence. Purchasers in the ordinary course of business take free of the lien imposed. The section does not, however, appear to be applicable to financing the dairy herd, since merchandise is defined to include only items intended for sale. Dairy cattle are not generally included in that category, certainly not at the time that they are made subject to a mortgage.

The supplemental mortgage and the annual new mortgage which are common in present practices lessen the risk that the security will diminish to but a few cattle. However, the freedom to sell the cattle and the freedom to use the proceeds thereof subject the lender to those same risks discussed in the section on crops —the risk of having the mortgage declared fraudulent against purchasers or creditors. An additional problem arises in the use of the supplemental mortgage or new mortgage to the extent that it secures prior advances covered by the initial mortgage. Thus those agencies which take a new mortgage each year covering all property, new and old, check the files of the register of deeds to ascertain the existence of any intervening third party rights against the property to be included in their mortgage. If such rights are properly filed they leave their original mortgage on record. If no rights are on file, some of the agencies satisfy the old mortgage at the time the new one is filed.

Judging from general principles of security law it is reasonable to conclude that the lender does not lose any of his rights by virtue of his satisfaction of the old mortgage when the new one is placed on file. The caution taken may in fact be unnecessary. The lender's prior rights in those cattle covered by the old mortgage and also included in the new one would date from the filing time of the original mortgage. This is in accordance with the doctrine that the lien of a refinancing mortgage dates back to the filing of the original.[25] The lender would be subrogated to all the rights which he had under the original mortgage at the time it was satisfied. Those rights, however, would include an interest only in those cattle covered by both the old and the new mortgage. Only to that extent would his priority date back to original filing.

As to the new cattle on the new mortgage or those on the supplemental mortgage, the lender's rights are somewhat less. Those cattle are in part security for a debt created prior to the time that they were subjected to the mortgage. Since a mortgage for a pre-existing debt is valid in Wisconsin so far as the parties themselves are concerned,[26] the new mortgage or supplemental mortgage improves the rights of the lender as against the borrower in that it covers the replacements and increases the cushion of security. It does not, however, necessarily improve the position of the lender as against third parties.

The case of *Funk* v. *Paul* [27] demonstrates the above statement. The case is important also because the language of the court provides the basis for the practice of specifically including increase in the mortgage.[28] The controversy arose over a mortgage from Gleim to the defendant on six milk cows to secure a present advance. Four of the cows were with calf at the time the mortgage was given. After the calves were born Gleim gave a mortgage on the calves to the plaintiff to secure a pre-existing debt not yet due. Both mortgages were placed on record on the day they were given. On the question of the best right to the calves the court held for the defendant—the owner of the mortgage on the cows—on the following grounds:

(1) As between the mortgagor and the mortgagee of the cows the mortgage on the cows included the increase thereof though increase was not specifically mentioned in the mortgage.

(2) Inasmuch as the calves were not specifically mentioned in the mortgage, third parties would not be apprised of the fact that the calves were covered by the mortgage, at least not after the calves ceased to follow the mother. Thus a subsequent bona fide purchaser or mortgagee of the calves would ordinarily prevail over a mortgagee of the cows.

(3) But the defendant—the mortgagee of the calves—was not a bona fide mortgagee because his mortgage was taken to secure a pre-existing obligation not then due.

It is clear that the language of the court to the effect that third parties were not apprised of the mortgagee's rights in the calves established the practice in Wisconsin of specifically including increase in the livestock mortgage. The effect of the court's decision on the use of the supplemental or new mortgage, however, is not entirely clear. Does the fact that a mortgagee for a pre-existing debt cannot claim as a bona fide purchaser for value mean that his rights may be defeated by an unfiled prior interest in the same property? If so, the lender in our new mortgage may not acquire any rights in the new or replacement cattle as against prior intervening lienholders whether they file or not. Similarly, the supplemental mortgage will not secure any of the pre-existing debt as against prior third party claimants.

Funk v. *Paul* suggests an affirmative answer to the question posed insofar as it says that a mortgagee for a pre-existing debt acquires no greater rights than those the mortgagor possessed.[29] Nonetheless, an argument can be made for the holder of the new or supplemental mortgage even as to the new cattle covered. Although the point was not argued in *Funk* v. *Paul,* the Wisconsin statute did not then and does not now say that an unfiled mortgage is invalid only against subsequent *purchasers for value.* It does say that a mortgage of personal property is invalid against *any other person* [30] than the parties unless possession is delivered or a copy has been filed.[31] Since an unfiled mortgage is invalid against all third parties, should the question of purchaser for value even arise? The statute has had a literal interpretation. Before a 1949 amendment the court held that a later mortgage which was filed was prior in right to an earlier unfiled mortgage even though the later mortgagee knew of it.[32] Similarly, it has been held that an unfiled transfer intended as security is invalid against creditors whether the creditors have perfected their claim by levy or not.[33] The position of the supplemental mortgagee or the lender who takes a new mortgage is also improved to the extent that it is accompanied by a renewal of the obligation or is expressly given in consideration for a release of certain property from the mortgage.[34]

We can at least conclude from the above court rulings that even though economic considerations support a freedom in the farmer to cull the dairy herd, the lender who grants such freedom completely is permitting the total value of his security to diminish. He also risks the loss of his security against purchasers and creditors. Even if he restricts such freedom by the use of a supplemental or new mortgage, a risk, though diminished, is still suffered.

The proposed Uniform Commercial Code seems to recognize the economic considerations involved in the transaction and does a great deal to reduce the legal risk. Inasmuch as the lender is interested principally in having the replacements covered in the mortgage so as not to reduce the overall value of his security, he can, by the use of an after-acquired clause, cover all replacements, whether they are acquired by birth or purchase. Priority under an after-acquired clause will date from the perfection of the original security interest, except as against purchase money lenders, even though no new advance is made.[35] The Code also validates, as against creditors, an agreement which gives the debtor freedom of disposition.[36] It is quite probable that the secured lender will grant such freedom to the debtor even though in so doing he loses possible rights as against purchasers of the cattle.[37] He looks to repayment from the sale of milk rather than from the sale of cattle.[38]

Beef cattle and hogs—freedom of disposition

The same freedom which is given to the cash crop farmer to negotiate the sale of his crops is given to the farmer in marketing his beef cattle and hogs, but the cattle and hog buyers, in contrast to the tobacco buyers, have not adopted the practice of paying the mortgage directly. The farmer is given the proceeds, and the lender looks to him for payment. Again, the lender runs the risk of having his mortgage declared invalid as against the purchaser and other creditors.[39] It must be admitted that it is a risk which for the most part is recognized only by lawyers and arises only because of existing law. That is to say, the cases in the books force the conclusion that such free and easy use of the collateral on the part of the debtor invalidates the mortgage. In general, the lender is aware of the risk. Why then does he permit it? The answer seems to be in the economics of the situation. The lenders are not now suffering losses. Therefore, the practical solution which freedom of disposition in the debtor provides is tolerated. Perhaps if agriculture suffers a panic and the bankruptcy courts then apply existing law, which will have the effect of making the lenders unsecured creditors, the practices will change. Some lenders recall such losses in the 1930's, but those experiences are no longer fresh and the memory does not specifically attribute the losses to invalid security rights.

Equally applicable here are the comments made in the discussion of crop mortgages about whether the lender will, when the Code is adopted, expressly grant power to sell in the mortgage, thereby accepting instead a lien on the proceeds. The typical mortgage now in use makes no provision for proceeds of private sale by the debtor. It does cover indemnity proceeds received when diseased cattle are destroyed by order of public authority.[40]

3. SECURITY IN EQUIPMENT

Section 241.08 of the 1951 Wisconsin Statutes provides that a mortgage on personal property is invalid as against parties other than the mortgagor and mortgagee unless a copy is filed or possession of the property is delivered to the mortgagee. In contrast, the statute covering conditional sales, Section 122.05, provides that the contract is void as against purchasers or lien creditors unless a copy is filed within ten days after the making of the conditional sale. The conditional sales vendor thus has a ten-day secret lien, whereas the chattel mortgagee must act with more promptness.

The distinction between the two documents suggests a possible improvement in the use of the combination bill of sale–bank draft form used by Production Credit associations in financing equipment purchases. It will be recalled that the bank draft is issued in blank to the farmer who negotiates it to the dealer with the purchase price entered. Possession of the equipment is given to the farmer, and a bill of sale is executed by the dealer to the Production Credit association. Although the instrument as executed is a bill of sale, there are ample grounds for believing that it will be treated as a mortgage if put to a court test.[41] It is for security purposes, possession is taken and retained by the farmer, and the farmer acknowledges an obligation to the Production Credit association. If it is treated as a mortgage, it is invalid as against third parties, since the document is not placed on record. No notice of the rights of the Production Credit association is given until the farmer executes a mortgage on the item and the mortgage is placed on file. Presumably there is a lapse of time before this is done.

The circumstances suggest the possibility of using a conditional sales contract rather than the bill of sale. The Production Credit association could deliver the bank draft to the farmer, the farmer could negotiate the draft to the dealer, and at the same time the farmer could execute a conditional sales contract. The dealer in cashing the draft would then assign the contract to the Production Credit association. The contract would be valid against third parties for a period of ten days after execution even though not filed. By that time a mortgage could be executed to the Production Credit association to replace the conditional sales contract.

The proposed arrangement is not entirely free of suspicion. It might well be called a chattel mortgage, just as the presently used bill of sale, for the reason that the accompanying bank draft makes it apparent that a third party who is not the seller is doing the financing. Technically, then, it does not conform to the theory of a conditional sale which presupposes an agreement by the vendor to transfer title upon the performance of a condition—the payment of the purchase price.[42] It presupposes also that the vendor, rather than a third party, extends the credit. The court might thus call the proposal a loan transaction in fact and treat it as a mortgage rather than a conditional sales contract.[43] Yet an assignment by a conditional vendor to a credit agency does not render the instrument a chattel mortgage.[44] There is little difference in result between an agreement by which a credit agency agrees to purchase conditional sale paper from a dealer and the issuance of a bank draft prior to the transaction. In both cases a third party advances the credit.

The provisions for filing security interests in equipment under the proposed code require that a purchase-money security interest where the price is less than $2500 need not be filed unless the equipment is part of the realty or is a motor vehicle which must be licensed. Protection against certain third parties is thus given without filing.[45] However, the farmer who buys such equipment and uses it in his farming operation takes free of the security interest unless it is filed.[46]

The logic of the provision that security interests of this nature need not be filed apparently is that the free flow of goods from manufacturer to dealer to consumer outweighs the risk of the dealer securing an additional loan on the equipment from the local bank after the manufacturer has financed the initial sale to the dealer. Obviously it would necessitate burdensome filing and discharging of relatively short term loans. In many instances the manufacturer would be an out-of-state concern.

This logic notwithstanding, the effect of the provision is that when the local bank finances the sale of equipment to a farmer and takes as security that equipment—assuming a value of less than $2500—it need not file the usual statement. It will be protected except in those rare situations in which another farmer purchases the equipment for his operation. No reason suggests itself why the bank should not file notice of this interest as well as an interest in the dairy herd or the like. The protection of third party purchasers and lenders is as important in equipment sales as in the sale of any other type of farm property. In the interest of facilitating dealer financing the draftsmen of the Code have apparently overlooked the further problem of financing the farmer in his purchases of equipment.

4. THE MILK CHECK ASSIGNMENT IN OPERATION

The necessity for a contract between the farmer and the creamery to support a valid milk check assignment was noted in the previous chapter. It accounts for the use of those forms which create such a contract. By the use of such a contract the claim of the lender is superior to that of a garnishing creditor, and, further, the lender is protected against attempted revocation by the debtor of the lender's right to collect funds due for milk delivered under the contract. The growth and use of the contract suggests that prior to its development such losses occurred often enough to cause concern to lenders and their lawyers.

A question may still arise if the farmer changes to another creamery before the loan is paid. Although the problem arises less often in recent years because the large centralized creamery or condensery is replacing the small cheese factory, it still happens often enough to make the lender aware of this particular risk. Such a change on the part of the farmer would give rise to a claim for damages on the part of the creamery, but such a claim would not solve the lender's problem. Apart from the coöperatives, which are entitled to specific performance of their marketing contracts by statute,[47] the creamery would probably not be entitled to specific performance. This is true because the creamery would have difficulty showing that this particular milk was essential to the economic operation of the plant and that milk of like quantity or quality could not be procured within a reasonable radius.[48] In fact, it probably could be shown that the only contracts for delivery that the creamery had were those which existed because lenders insisted on them before taking assignments. This free and easy way of dealing with the majority of its producers would hardly sustain a claim by the creamery of economic necessity that all milk from each producer continue to reach the plant.

The assignment of proceeds coupled with the contract makes the lender a beneficiary of the contract between the farmer and the creamery in that such contract gives existence to the fund which is assigned. This is particularly true in those forms by which the creamery expressly agrees to deliver the proceeds to the lender rather than just accept the assignment. The lender thus has from the creamery a promise to deliver funds otherwise due the debtor.

Because of this relationship, what remedies does the lender have in the event the farmer fails to deliver his milk to the creamery? The express promise of the creamery to pay over proceeds would avail the lender nothing. It is impliedly conditioned on continued performance by the farmer. If the farmer fails to perform, the creamery is released.[49] The lender's sole remedy would then be against the farmer, and as a practical matter the only worthwhile remedy would be to compel the farmer to deliver milk to the creamery in accordance with his existing contract or to compel him to enter into a new contract with the new creamery and then execute an assignment of that fund to the lender.

The granting of such remedy would be, if at all, under the equity powers of a court. It can be argued that the lender has a security right in an account receivable arising from the contract to deliver milk coupled with the assignment of the proceeds thereof.[50] Does this existence of a security right mean that a court of equity will intervene to protect the lender's right to the proceeds of the milk?

A possible basis for answering the question in the affirmative might be the theory that although equity would not enforce the contract for the creamery because damages at law are adequate, payment in damages is not an adequate remedy for the lender. A similar result is reached under the equity powers of the court whenever a party promises to give security for an obligation due another.[51] Clearly, damages in money will not be an adequate remedy for a failure to perform such a promise. There is in this relationship already a right to recover money by virtue of the indebtedness. An additional right to recover money damages does not give the lender security for that indebtedness.

A court of equity could also reason that the farmer's contract with the creamery gives existence to a fund. This fund is then assigned to the lender. Because of the contract which creates the fund and the assignment thereof the lender is induced to loan money. Implicit in the relationship is a continuing promise on the part of the lender to act so as to give a continued existence to the fund. A change of creamery violates this obligation, and unless the farmer is forced to perform his contract with the creamery the lender is without an adequate remedy. It is then not unlike a promise to give security which, as we have noted, equity will enforce.

A possible argument against a court of equity enforcing the contract between the farmer and the creamery at the suit of the lender might be that although equity will enforce a promise to give security the promise here is not to give security but merely to deliver milk. The argument is one of form, not of substance. The answers to it are twofold. The first is alluded to in the paragraph above; that is, the promise is a continuing one, a promise to deliver milk for a fixed period of time to secure the lender for a loan given.

The second argument is that the act of discontinuing delivery to the creamery which holds the assignment impairs the security which the lender has, since in the absence of delivery there are no proceeds to which the assignment can attach. In the debtor's delivery of his milk to a new creamery, there is no contract to give existence to a fund, an element vital to assignments of proceeds under Wisconsin law. Because the act of refusing delivery to the creamery which holds the assignment impairs the security interest of the lender, will not a court of equity grant an injunction to prevent such impairment? The remedy at law is not adequate. Money damages for breach will not give the lender protection against other claimants to the proceeds of the milk sold. This remedy is analogous to the power of a court of equity to enjoin the mortgagor from committing waste to the mortgaged premises at the suit of the mortgagee. A mortgagor may be restrained from cutting timber on mortgaged land if such act impairs the security of the mortgagee; [52] a land contract vendor may enjoin the removal of fixtures if it impairs the security.[53] The theory supporting this line of cases is that the proposed act of the borrower will impair the security of the lender; a remedy of money damages is not adequate; and therefore equity will intervene to prevent the act. The theory is indeed applicable when the farmer threatens to break his contract to deliver milk to the creamery.

The weakness of the foregoing arguments is that a court would hesitate to undertake the supervision necessary to enforce such an order.[54] Enforcement would mean that the court would be forcing a farmer to continue doing business with a creamery to which he does not want to sell not because the creamery insisted on it but because the bank's security is in jeopardy. It would be simpler to order the farmer to execute another assignment. But this would not solve the problem. There would be no contract between the farmer and the new creamery, and the contract is necessary to make the assignment valid. Although the bank could order the farmer to execute a new contract, it cannot so order the new creamery because, of course, the new creamery is not a party to the suit and is under no legal obligation to enter into such a contract.

If a court does not require performance of the original contract, the bank is without a secured right. If it does enforce the contract, it is doing so only for the purpose of assuring the lender a secured right in the proceeds of the milk. Thus we find a court of equity enforcing a contract not because the parties themselves insist but only because they have previously said that an assignment of proceeds to become due is not valid unless there is a contract to deliver, which contract gives existence to a fund.[55] The same result could have been reached by recognizing in the first instance that the assignment is itself a continuing promise, enforceable in equity, to give security by assigning the proceeds of the milk as delivered.[56] There would then be no need for a contract which now exists solely for the purpose of giving existence to a fund which avoids the court-made rule that you cannot transfer that which you do not have or which is not in existence.

As has been noted in Chapter II, the proposed Uniform Commercial Code contemplates a security interest in a contract right or in an account and allows future accounts to be assigned as security. The existing practice is not to file the milk check assignment. No statute provides for such filing. Under the Code the lender would have to file a financing statement to perfect his interest as against third parties.[57]

If a statement is properly filed, the holder of a security interest in milk accounts will be entitled to priority from the date of filing. The difficulties of priority—difficulties noted in discussing crops to be grown—are not ordinarily present here since the milk check which the farmer receives is usually in payment of milk delivered more than two weeks prior to the date of the check. At any particular time selected there is money due the farmer. An account as such is always in existence, and the debtor has present rights in it. The security interest therefore attaches when the agreement is made,[58] and the priority as to future accounts dates from the time of original perfection, which in this case is identical with the time of filing.[59]

Under the Code the lender who relies on the proceeds of future milk deliveries as security will not have his security rights affected by the farmer's change of creamery. By providing for an interest in present and future milk accounts, the lender acquires an interest in future sales of milk by the farmer regardless of the purchaser. Since an account is defined as a right to payment for goods sold,[60] a contract right may become an account when goods are delivered and the right to payment accrues. Even if a contract right rather than an account is assigned, there is apparently no reason why future contracts for payment for milk deliveries cannot be included in the assignment. So, too, if the contract with the original creamery is modified or a new contract is substituted the lender gets corresponding rights in the contract.[61]

5. Field-warehousing arrangements

Ordinarily a pledge of property for security contemplates delivery of the property to the secured lender and his retention of it until the debt is paid. The arrangement obviously is unsuited to most farm credit arrangements because the farm personal property on which a loan is made is essential to production.

The reason for the requirement of delivery under the pledge is not only to place in the lender's hands tangible property which he can sell to repay the debt but also to apprise third persons of the fact that someone other than the debtor has specific rights in the property pledged. The validity of the field-warehousing arrangement depends upon the extent to which the property is effectively placed beyond the control of the debtor and the extent to which third parties are advised of the lender's rights. The arrangement made by the canning company cited in Chapter II will be recalled. In this transaction the canning company delivers property to an agent of the warehouse company for storage on the canner's premises, where it is separated from other property and designated by lot number. The agent selected is usually also an employee of the canner.

Two aspects of this arrangement are suspect, though they do not necessarily invalidate it. The fact that the goods are kept on the premises of the canner rebuts the notion of the pledge which contemplates delivery to the lender. However, the delivery to a third person for the lender is approved, and the goods may be stored on the premises of the debtor if proper precautions are taken. These precautions consist of separating the pledged goods from those not pledged, denying the debtor access to or control of the pledged goods, and posting adequate signs stating that the property and that portion of the premises is in the possession of the warehouse company.[62] The fact that the agent is also an employee of the canner tends to rebut the denial of access or control in the canner. A banker with whom this situation was discussed was not too concerned about the dual employment of the agent or about the fact that the separation was not as complete as it might be.[63] He relied heavily on the bond of the warehouse company.

Under the proposed code, pledging of goods under a field-warehouse arrangement will not be perfected, that is, valid against purchasers or creditors, unless notice is given by filing.[64] There is some feeling on the part of field-warehousemen that their services will no longer be necessary with the adoption of the Code inasmuch as the after-acquired provisions [65] and the provision validating a freedom of disposition in the debtor [66] will permit a floating lien on inventory of the debtor and will give the debtor the right to use and make replacements in the security in the ordinary course of his business.[67]

The Code generally adopts the common law notions of the pledge by recognizing that possession by a lender perfects a security interest without filing.[68] The lender in possession has a duty of reasonable care in the custody and preservation of the collateral.[69]

6. Landlord-tenant protection of rights of landlords

Although the case of *Layng* v. *Stout* [70] recognized as valid the interest of a landlord in future crops grown by his tenant, the court suggested that when the crops were severed the landlord might by his actions estop himself from claiming the crop against a bona fide purchaser.[71] He can by implication make the tenant his agent for the purpose of selling the crop.

The court's language in defining the rights of innocent purchasers probably accounted for the not unusual practice of filing such leases as chattel security documents in Wisconsin. Presumably, however, even though he files the landlord might estop himself against a purchaser. Certainly, freedom to sell or use the crop would belie the landlord's claim of title against third parties.[72] It seems reasonable to conclude that it was not the failure to file that the court referred to in the Layng case but rather the freedom of disposition impliedly granted.[73] Inasmuch as no statute in Wisconsin provides for filing, the landlord could successfully argue that in the absence of a filing provision the common law rule of first in time, first in right, should prevail. Filing is not the issue. In contrast, the Wisconsin Statutes do provide for filing the cropper's contract to give notice of the owner's sole title to the crop.[74] The owner forfeits his rights in the crop against third parties by his failure to file the contract. Then third parties are entitled to treat the parties to the cropper contract as landlord and tenant and thus as owners of an undivided one-half interest in the crop. The filing provision was added in 1947. It is still new enough to find owners who have suffered a loss of one-half of their crop because of ignorance of the statute and resulting failure to file.[75]

Under the proposed code, the title retention lease must be filed to protect the landlord's interest just as any other security interest. Even then it may, during the term of the lease, become subordinate to the interest of a lender whose loan enables the debtor to produce the crop to the extent that the security interest described in the lease secures rent more than six months due at the time the crop is planted. To take priority in this situation the production loan must be made either during the particular production season or not more than three months before the crop is planted.[76]

7. AGREEMENTS FOR FUTURE ADVANCES

Largely as a result of the impetus provided by the Production Credit association, it is increasingly common for financing agencies to arrange for the satisfaction of a farmer's entire credit needs by making advances as needed and by accepting payments as the farmer can make them. The practice is commonly referred to as a budget loan. Considerable freedom is given to the farmer in making changes in his property or in selling his produce. When new property is acquired the agency generally prefers that it be covered by the mortgage.

The plan poses problems of a security interest in after-acquired property and of securing future advances. The after-acquired problem is handled, as noted previously, by powers of attorney to execute a mortgage and by the use of the supplemental mortgage. The future advance problem is usually handled by a clause in the mortgage which provides that the property described shall secure certain executed notes and all future advances up to a named sum.[77] Some agencies, by far the minority, provide for all future advances without naming a top figure.[78]

In addition to the budget loan, one other method of handling the future advance problem was encountered—this one in connection with financing the production of turkeys. The turkey farmer needs money to purchase the poults originally and then greater sums as the season progresses to purchase feed for them. The initial advance needed to purchase the poults may be unsecured or secured by other property. After the poults are acquired the farmer signs a note for the amount that will be needed over the entire season and secures it by a mortgage on the turkeys. At that time the only money that the bank has advanced is the purchase price, and this sum is secured by the turkeys. As the season progresses, the bank advances additional money to pay for the necessary feed. Meanwhile the turkeys are becoming more valuable, and thus the cushion of security increases with the advances.

These additional advances are handled in a three-way transaction between the farmer, the feed dealer, and the bank. When the farmer purchases feed from the dealer, he signs an invoice which authorizes the bank to pay the dealer the invoice price out of the proceeds of the note which the farmer has signed.[79]

It is difficult to ascertain the reasons for the use of the closed-end–future-advance clause in Wisconsin. Perhaps this is evidence of business caution on the part of most lenders. They do not wish to generate a belief on the part of the borrower that credit is unlimited. Because of the emphasis placed on the written word, this provision may have a psychological advantage. The only limitation placed by the Wisconsin court on the priority of future advances as against third parties is that the mortgage must indicate that future advances are contemplated.[80] Presumably even that provision would be unnecessary if the parties knew the amount of the intended advance and made the note and mortgage for that amount.

There is evidence that the lender believes that by naming a top figure he will have priority to that amount as against third parties regardless of the conditions surrounding the future advance. The Wisconsin court has not decided this issue precisely. However, the general rule in the United States would not support such a conclusion. Subsequent optional advances—that is, the granting of additional funds by the lender in the absence of an obligation to make future advances—are subordinated to the lien of a subsequent mortgage if they are made after the first lender has received actual notice of the second encumbrance. The issue is whether the advances are optional or obligatory, not whether a top sum has been named.[81]

A future advance may be declared obligatory if the advance is necessary to protect the security which the lender already has,[82] if there is an enforceable contract to make a total advance, or if the full amount is charged against the debtor.[83] Among the practices discovered, only the turkey loan arrangement suggests an obligatory advance. Here the debtor signs a note for the full amount contemplated in the transaction during the season. In the other instances in which the clause is used there are no advances contemplated at the time. The future advance is only a possibility.

The basic controversy involved in any discussion of future advance clauses is the method by which third parties are able to ascertain the amount of the obligation secured. Should they be able to determine this by looking at the record? or should it be sufficient if the record directs them to sources of information? The filing provisions of the proposed code are based on the theory that notice filing is adequate. The filed statement need only inform the record searcher of the existence of a security interest. The amount of the obligation is not an essential part of the financing statement.[84]

A provision for future advances in the security agreement is expressly approved by the Code,[85] and priority for all advances dates from the time that the security interest is originally perfected.[86] Implicit in this provision is a change in existing law which gives priority only for advances made prior to actual notice of a second encumbrance unless there is an obligation to make such additional allowances. This change may work harshly on some debtors. If the first lender takes a security interest in all of the debtor's property to secure present and future advances but refuses to make an additional advance when it is needed, a second lender cannot safely make an advance even though the first lender has more than adequate security. The debtor's hope for additional financing depends then upon his ability to find a lender who will advance sufficient credit to pay off the first lender as well as to meet the debtor's additional need. There is, then, in this situation a clear opportunity to subject debtors to the economic will of the first lender. Such lenders can, by offering or withholding advances, pretty much determine the course of action to be followed. The debtor in turn is helpless to get funds from another party. The second lender cannot run the risk of being subordinated to any and all advances of the first lender, and, further, if the agreement includes an after-acquired clause, the debtor's entire assets will be tied to the first loan.

CHAPTER FOUR

Enforcement of the security where debtor defaults

1. WHERE THE LENDER IS IN POSSESSION UNDER A PLEDGE

Although no evidence of actual foreclosure of property pledged was discovered in the course of this investigation, certain provisions for such action in the forms in use deserve comment. These provisions state that the lender may, at his option, sell the collateral pledged at public or private sale without prior notice to the debtor and that the lender himself may purchase at the sale. The power may be exercised whether or not the obligation secured has matured, and it may be exercised without prior demand for payment. One form further provides that the bank may have the pledged stocks transferred to its own name and that the bank need take no steps to realize on the collateral.[1]

At common law the lender in possession of pledged property was permitted an out of court sale to realize on his security. Certain restrictions on such action were established, however, to protect the debtor. It was felt that he should have notice of the sale to enable him to redeem or secure a purchaser. The sale had to be public and had to be held after public notice. These rules were designed to assure a fair sale. The sale had to be held after default, and the purchaser could not purchase at the sale.[2]

Although courts have insisted on these rules, they have in turn rendered most of them nugatory by recognizing that the debtor may waive certain of the protections in the pledge agreement. The debtor may consent to a private sale;[3] he may waive notice of any proposed sale;[4] and he may consent to a purchase of the collateral by the lender.[5] The contract provisions, being contrary to court-made doctrine, are, however, strictly construed. For example, a grant of a power of sale does not amount to a consent giving the lender the right to purchase.[6] There seems to be little doubt that the debtor may waive the requirement of a public sale, the notice thereof, and that he may consent to a purchase by the lender, all of which he does in the forms used.

However, it is apparent from the cases that any sale of the collateral must be for a fair price. The sale of the pledged property is always subject to attack on this ground. The provision that the lender may sell before maturity is also suspect. Such provisions are strictly construed. In *National Bank of Illinois* v. *Baker,*[7] the court in construing a provision authorizing a sale before maturity in the event of a decline in market value of the security [8] held that the debtor was entitled to notice of such proposed sale even though a waiver of notice provision was included in the agreement. The waiver of notice was said to be applicable to a sale after maturity but not before. The court reasoned that when the debtor knows the maturity date he has an opportunity to redeem beforehand, but when a sale is held before maturity and notice thereof is not given, the debtor has no reason to suspect that his interest may be cut off and no opportunity to redeem the property.

The other notable provisions in the forms giving the bank power to transfer the securities to its own name and absolving the bank of the need for taking steps to realize on the security are not clear. If they mean that the bank may on default hold the property in satisfaction of the debt without a sale, they are invalid.[9] If, on the other hand, the provision discharging the bank from responsibility for taking steps to realize on the property means that the privilege of the bank to proceed on the obligation without

selling the collateral is preserved, there is no doubt that the bank
has this power.[10]

2. Where the debtor is in possession

What the law says—the foreclosure remedies provided

Section 241.13 of the Wisconsin Statutes provides in detail for
an out-of-court foreclosure of a chattel mortgage.[11] Again, however, the elaborate procedure provided by law is often in sharp
contrast with what actually happens when lenders find it necessary to rely on the security to satisfy their claims. According to
law, the following steps are necessary.

The first step in the process is optional with the mortgagee. He
may or may not serve upon the mortgagor a notice of intent to
seize the property which secures the debt. However, unless a ten-
day written notice is served, no costs of taking or keeping the property pending sale may be collected. This notice of intent to seize is
generally not given, principally because the mortgagee feels that
such advance notice will cause the debtor to conceal or dispose
of the property. If it is given it is sent by registered mail as part
of a request for payment of the loan, and the intent to seize is
stated conditionally in words such as these: "Unless payment is
made within ten days from the receipt of this letter we will be
forced to pick up the property, etc."

After the property has been seized by the mortgagee it may
not be removed from the county in which it was taken. Thereafter, and at least ten days before the contemplated sale, the mortgagee must serve a notice of the proposed sale on the debtor if he
resides within the county and on any junior mortgagee whose
mortgage is filed.[12] If the mortgagee intends to sue for a deficiency
he must state this fact on the notice of sale.

During this ten-day period the debtor, or those claiming under
him, may redeem the property by paying the mortgage debt and
the costs of taking, assuming that a notice of intent to seize is
given; otherwise they may claim just the amount of the debt. The
sale may be either public or private. If it is public the mortgagor
has the privilege of selecting the auctioneer. According to statute,
this auctioneer shall be paid by the mortgagor and shall have no
claim on the proceeds of the sale except that portion which may
be in excess of the obligation owed.

After the sale is completed, and within ten days thereafter, the mortgagee or his agent must file an affidavit of sale setting forth the costs, expenses, and proceeds of the sale.[13] If the proceeds of the sale are not adequate to satisfy the obligation and if the notice of sale included a declaration to seek a deficiency judgment, the mortgagee may thereafter get such judgment. This can be accomplished, however, only in an action brought for that purpose. In such action the court is directed to find the reasonable value of the chattels sold and base its deficiency on this figure rather than on the sale price.[14]

The provision for notice of the foreclosure sale as set forth in Section 241.13 may not be waived by the debtor; at least, according to the language of the provision, no act or agreement at the time or before the making of the contract or statement in the contract shall constitute a waiver of such protection. Anyone aggrieved by a violation may recover twenty-five dollars plus actual damages. Any sale held without notice or before the period of redemption prescribed shall amount to a payment of the debt and a cancellation of the mortgage.[15] The provisions of the deficiency statute—Section 241.134—may not be waived except by written agreement for consideration after default.

Sections 122.16 through 122.26 of the Wisconsin Statutes relate to the foreclosure of the conditional sales contract. Any breach of the contract which is expressly made grounds for retaking the property authorizes a taking of possession. The retaking shall be by peaceful means if possible, otherwise by legal process. In no event may household goods be retaken without legal process. Again, the owner of the contract has an election to give or not give a notice of intention to retake. No penalty, such as a denial of the costs, results from the failure to give such a notice when a conditional sales contract is involved. If it is given, however—not more than forty nor less than twenty days prior to the retaking— the right of the purchaser to redeem the goods is cut off at the end of this period by the taking, and thereafter the goods may be removed from the state. If the notice of intent to retake is not given, the contract owner must keep the goods within the state for a period of ten days after seizure, during which time the purchaser may redeem the goods and continue under the contract.

According to those who use the conditional sales contract as much and often as possible, the above factors are its great advantages. That is, lenders do not lose costs by failure to give a notice of intent to seize, and they may take repossessed goods anywhere within the state. Again, as in the case of the chattel mortgage, the notice of intent to seize is seldom given, though such notice, if otherwise safe, does have the great advantage of cutting off the debtor's right to redeem before seizure rather than after.

If at the time of retaking less than 50 per cent of the purchase price has been paid, and if the buyer does not redeem within ten days after the retaking, the lender may retain the goods. Such retention releases the buyer from all obligations. However, the buyer may insist that a sale of the goods be held. If more than 50 per cent of the purchase price has been paid, the seller must sell the repossessed goods at public auction in the state where they were at the time of retaking. Such sale, if compulsory, must be within thirty days after retaking or, if demanded by the buyer, within thirty days after the demand. Notice of the sale must be given the buyer in writing ten days before the sale, copies of the notice must be posted five days before the sale, and if five hundred dollars has been paid on the purchase price, notice of the sale must be published in a newspaper at least five days before the sale.

If the proceeds of the sale are not adequate to satisfy the obligation, the seller may recover a deficiency in an action brought for that purpose. This deficiency is based on the reasonable value of the goods sold rather than on the sale price.

The penalty provisions for failure of the lender to comply with the sale requirements give the buyer the right to recover actual damages and in no event less than one-fourth of the payments made. No act or agreement before or at the time of the making of the contract constitutes a valid waiver of the provisions set forth for the resale except that the contract may provide for rescission in case of breach of the terms of the contract. Such rescission must be accompanied by crediting the buyer with the full purchase price of the goods so retaken. The protective provisions of the deficiency judgment section may be waived by the buyer by written agreement for consideration.

Judging from the detailed steps required by statute in realizing on chattel securities it is evident that the legislature had in mind as important objectives adequate notice to the debtor and opportunity to redeem the property. These protective provisions are not to be waived by the debtor, and such waiver if given is recog-

nized as oppressive and declared invalid.[16] Penalties are imposed
on the lender who does not comply, and the penalty is usually at
least a cancellation of the balance due—that is, a denial of any
deficiency. It may well be more than this.

What actually happens—the voluntary surrender

It was ironic to discover in the course of this investigation that
this careful legislation designed to protect the debtor is seldom
used. Not a single banker interviewed could recall a statutory foreclosure of chattel property. Lawyers interviewed could recall only
a few instances of such foreclosure, and they usually related to
something other than farm personalty. Even the finance companies, who deal principally with high risk debtors, do not have
many.

Part of this, of course, can be attributed to the good financial
condition of farmers in recent years. But that is not all of the story.
The statutory foreclosure is used with the so-called "dead beat"
who refuses to cooperate. Most debtors recognize that statutory
foreclosure is not necessarily in their best interests. It is expensive,
and it does not usually bring the fair value of the goods. Public
sales are inclined to attract only bargain hunters and bids are
chilled. Debtors, therefore, are willing to cooperate with the lender
in getting out from under the debt as painlessly as possible.

A popular method of accomplishing this is the "voluntary surrender." This consists of an agreement between the lender and the
debtor whereby the debtor delivers the property to the lender
with the understanding that the lender will sell the property at
private sale and apply the proceeds on the obligation. The debtor
is entitled to the excess, if any, and the lender reserves the right
to sue for a deficiency if one remains. This agreement is often oral,
though at least one agency had a specific form for the purpose.
This particular agency has recently revised the form in use. The
basic difference is that the revised form provides for express waiver
of the statutes regulating foreclosure sales, in consideration of
which the lender agrees to a 10 per cent reduction in any deficiency
which may remain.[17]

It is at least questionable whether this new form with its provision for genuine consideration is any solution. True, the statute
contemplates an agreement for consideration insofar as the procedure for a deficiency is concerned.[18] The procedure authorized

by the voluntary surrender not only waives the court valuation proceedings in a suit for a deficiency but also alters the sale procedures which precede such suit. The statute indicates that these latter provisions cannot be waived by agreement.[19]

A definite answer to the validity of the practice cannot be stated on the basis of present case law on the subject. An early case, *Welcome* v. *Mitchell*,[20] involved a contest between a purchaser at a private sale of mortgaged property held without compliance with a statute regulating foreclosure sale and levying creditors of the mortgagor. The court in upholding the title of the purchaser said that the statute was designed to protect the mortgagor, that he might waive the benefit thereof, and that his creditors could not attack the sale. The statute involved, however, was Chapter 294, Laws of 1887, which provided in part that "no sale . . . *except by consent of the mortgagor* [21] shall be made before the expiration of five days."

In *Vreeland* v. *Waddell*,[22] decided under the same statute, the court held that an authorization in the mortgage that the mortgagee might sell the property without notice did not amount to a waiver of the provision for holding the property for five days after seizure.[23]

Hammel v. *Cairnes* [24] involved the failure of the mortgagee to file an affidavit of foreclosure sale. The sale did not bring sufficient funds to satisfy the indebtedness. In a subsequent action for deficiency the mortgagor claimed that the failure to file an affidavit was a forfeiture of the balance due. The court held that there was no forfeiture because the defendant surrendered the property to the mortgagee voluntarily and this was not a taking as contemplated by the statute.[25]

In 1939, the statute was amended to exclude the provisions for consent by the mortgagor.[26] The statute, however, still refers to a sale of property *taken* [27] by virtue of a chattel mortgage. Presumably the amendment was intended to have the chattel mortgage statute conform to the conditional sales statute. The case of *Mack International Motor Truck Corp.* v. *Thelen Trucking Co.*,[28] decided in 1931, can be said to indicate the possible intention of the 1939 amendment to the chattel mortgage act. In this case the vendor took possession of certain trucks sold to the purchaser under a conditional sales contract. The vendor then advertised the trucks for sale, but the notice was served on the purchaser less than ten days prior thereto. The vendor then asked the purchaser to consent to a postponement of the sale until ten days after the notice. No further notice was given. In suing for a deficiency the vendor contended that such consent by the purchaser was a valid waiver of the prescribed notice. The court held that this protection could not be waived and that although the statute referred to an agreement at the time of the making of the contract, the spirit of the act extended to a subsequent agreement. The opinion of the court in part (p. 434) was as follows: "If we concede the right of the buyer to waive these requirements we will remove from the subject of the law's solicitude a protection which was designed for their benefit."

On the basis of the cases decided under the old statute, the subsequent amendment of the chattel mortgage statute, and the Mack International case, certain conclusions can be reached. The protective provisions relating to notice of sale, whether under a chattel mortgage or under a conditional sales contract, may not be waived by an agreement either in the original contract or by a subsequent waiver. The court will not, however, enforce the harsh penalty provisions of the chattel mortgage statute when the indebtedness remaining is far out of proportion to the actual damages of the mortgagor. Even though *Hammel* v. *Cairnes* [29] rationalized the refusal to enforce the penalty provisions on the ground that a voluntary surrender was not a taking, it was the penalty which was abhorrent to the court. The language "taken by virtue of" in the present statute does not mean that every voluntary surrender waives the provisions.

To state the conclusions another way, the use of the old form, without provision for a waiver for consideration, subjected the user thereof to the milder penalty provisions of the two acts—that is, actual damages of the mortgagor plus twenty-five dollars liquidated damages where a chattel mortgage is involved [30]—or in the case of a conditional sale, actual damages, but not less than one-fourth of the payments made. Further, if less than 50 per cent of the purchase price on a conditional sale contract is paid, the court would call the invalid sale no sale at all and declare the debt paid.

The reading of the statute suggests that a similar result should be reached even with the use of the new form which does provide for consideration. The deficiency judgment procedure calling for a court determination of the value of the goods may be waived for a consideration, but the notice of sale, including the time provisions, may not be waived by an agreement. Presumably this includes an agreement for which consideration is given. The only light found on the subject is a statement by the court in the Mack International Motor Truck case. Here the court quoted a New York case to the effect that a waiver or consent not in the form of a contract would frustrate the purpose of the legislature in protecting the debtor.[31] Apparently, any decision would depend upon the loss to the debtor—that is, whether a 10 per cent reduction of the deficiency was felt to be adequate for a denial of the opportunity to redeem and the opportunity to find a purchaser. The court would also look carefully at the circumstances surrounding the signing of the surrender agreement by the debtor to determine just how voluntary it was.

Some history relative to this change of forms by the one agency noted may well be of interest to the reader as a commentary on law and practice. The old form had been in existence for some time, and its use was supported on the theory that although the statutes prohibit a waiver at the time of, or before, the making of the contract, they did not prohibit a waiver entered into at a later date, presumably after default. It was further argued that there was in fact a consideration, which as stated in the form was that suit would not be brought. Thus, it was reasoned, the debtor was saved the humiliation of a foreclosure sale. Interestingly enough, the debtor was permitted to avoid humiliation by waiving certain statutes which presumably the legislature had enacted for his protection. In any event, the company never had the opportunity to argue the matter in court. A number of deficiency judgments were taken by virtue of the procedure authorized in the form, but in none of these cases did the defendants appear to contest the action by urging the foreclosure statute as a defense.

What actually happens—the voluntary auction sale

When all or much of the personal property of the farmer is subject to a mortgage and it becomes apparent that the farmer is not going to be able to refinance his indebtedness or keep up with the present mortgage, it is not unusual for the lender to encourage the debtor to sell his property at public auction. Every indication is given that this is a sale made entirely on the debtor's own initiative. The reason stated in the advertisement is usually "have decided to quit farming." Often enough, however, the circumstance leading to such a sale is heavy indebtedness. Both the lender and the debtor realize, of course, that a sale which is to all appearances voluntary will bring greater proceeds than the foreclosure sale. This suggests the need for a study of the public foreclosure and judicial sale as an institution with a view toward eliminating or reducing the effect of those elements which encourage chilled bidding.

The lender bank in a fair number of cases acts as the clerk at this auction. The proceeds come directly to it and are applied on the loan. Or an auction company may be employed to handle the sale and arrangements made for the auction company to deliver the proceeds to the bank or other lender.[32]

It seems quite clear that there is nothing in this arrangement which is a violation of the statutes relating to the foreclosure of secured chattel loans. The debtor never surrenders possession of the property. It can be fairly said that the bank or auction company is acting as his agent in selling the property, though the sale may materially benefit them.

Although the voluntary auction sale does not violate the foreclosure statutes, a legal problem does arise as to the right of the lender to the proceeds of the sale or to the property which is sold. The sale amounts to a privilege in the debtor to sell property subject to a mortgage. The legal effect of a grant of such power was discussed at length in Chapter III. The conclusions presented there were that such consent waived the mortgage lien as against the purchaser, that an indefinite agreement about the use of the proceeds might amount to a waiver of the mortgage security against other creditors, and that any freedom in the debtor to use the proceeds made the mortgage invalid as against third parties.

This problem of waiver of security by giving permission to sell is faced by the banker in various ways. One way of facing it, or, more accurately, of not facing it, is for the banker to have nothing to do with the sale and to carefully abstain from attending it. If there is trouble, the bank then claims there was no consent to the sale, that it was without its knowledge. A banker interviewed in the course of this investigation seemed unaware that even while he was strongly supporting this position a poster announcing such an auction sale was hanging in the lobby of his bank. But most lenders do not take this ostrich-like attitude. One of the reasons they do not is a line of case law authorities supporting a more realistic approach to the auction sale transaction.

The court has been much kinder to the institution of the auction sale as a mortgagee's remedy than to a surrender of the property to the lender without public sale. In *Black Hawk State Bank* v. *Accola*,[33] a mortgagee with an improperly filed mortgage agreed with his debtor to an auction sale. There was an order from the debtor directing the auctioneer to deliver the proceeds to the mortgagee. A creditor garnished the funds in the hands of the auctioneer. The court in holding for the mortgagee said that although the improperly filed mortgage subjected the property to claims of attaching creditors, the agreement for the auction plus the order to the auctioneer was an equitable assignment of the funds.[34]

This position was affirmed in *Caroline State Bank* v. *Andrews* [35] in which the court recognized that a mortgagee who authorizes a mortgagor to sell waives his lien but said there was no such waiver if the mortgagee directs the purchaser to pay him rather than the mortgagor. In *Carpenter* v. *Forbes*,[36] the debtor, O. Forbes, was indebted to Helmenstine on a chattel mortgage, to S. Forbes on a junior mortgage, and to Allen and Salzman, unsecured creditors. O. Forbes arranged an auction sale and hired Gray as auctioneer. O. Forbes then assigned the property to Allen and Salzman subject to the first mortgage. The assignment was accompanied by an oral agreement that the property was to be sold, the expenses paid, the first mortgage, then Allen and Salzman, and finally S. Forbes paid. S. Forbes, the second mortgagee, agreed to this arrangement. The sale was held, the expenses paid, and the first mortgagee was paid. At that point the funds were garnished by the plaintiff. The court in ruling against the garnishing creditor recognized that the assignment of the property to Allen and Salzman was an invalid mortgage because there was no change in possession and no filing. Citing *Caroline State Bank* v. *Andrews,* the court held that S. Forbes did not waive his mortgage lien because his consent to the sale was on the condition that the proceeds be delivered to Gray and then to him. The court held further that, in any event, the agreement between the debtor, the secured creditors, the unsecured creditors, and the auctioneer was an equitable assignment giving the assignees a secured right.

This triumph of form over substance was reiterated by the

court in *Aamodt* v. *Bergren.*[37] Here the debtor gave a bill of sale
of the property to be sold to the creditor. The creditor delivered
the bill of sale to the auction company. In holding for another
creditor who garnished the funds in the hands of the auction company, the court said that the bill of sale was an invalid chattel
mortgage because it was not filed; that it was therefore invalid
against creditors; and that it did not operate as an equitable assignment because there was no direction to the auctioneer to pay
the holder of the bill of sale.

Apparently, therefore, chattel mortgages and bills of sale, the
formal documents, will not preserve the creditors' rights, but the
simple assignment of proceeds will. Hence, if you are a secured
creditor and give your consent to an auction sale, the consent is
not a waiver of your security rights, if your consent is conditional
on the delivery of the proceeds of the sale to you and the auctioneer
is so advised.[38] Even if you are an unsecured creditor and get an
assignment of the proceeds to you, you will be preferred over other
creditors who do not have such an assignment.

As has been stated, this line of authority has meant that most of
the credit agencies do not take the ostrich-like attitude of the
banker referred to above in handling the auction sale. Rather, a
set of practices and forms has evolved in recognition of the case
law on the subject.

Where the lender is clerking the sale, a form called an assignment of sale proceeds is used. This is an agreement between the
creditor and the debtor approving the sale and assigning the proceeds but retaining the security lien on all chattels not sold.[39]
Where a third party is clerking the sale, one of the forms used is
more emphatic in stating that the owner of the security interest
relinquishes his lien to the purchasers at the sale.[40] In turn, the
owner assigns sufficient of the proceeds to satisfy the lien after the
payment of expenses. This form was drawn by an auction company not a party to the loan and was designed especially to protect
the auctioneer.

The other form discovered in the survey is perhaps the most
direct, though not necessarily the best. It is designed for property
subject to a chattel mortgage and provides that the auction sale,
at the instance of the debtor, shall be a substitute for a foreclosure
sale. To this end the debtor waives notice of the sale by publication
and also waives the filing of a report. The secured lender waives

nothing, but he does consent to the sale on the condition that the proceeds be delivered to him. The waiver of notice by publication in the form is interesting, since there is no provision for publication of the notice of foreclosure sale in Wisconsin.[41] There is a provision for serving the notice on the debtor, but this is not specifically waived in the form. This can perhaps be explained by the fact that the form is sold by a Minnesota stationer.[42] Nonetheless it is in use in Wisconsin.

What actually happens—criminal sanctions

There is reason to believe that the "voluntary" surrender and the "voluntary" auction sale are not in all instances voluntary. In the majority of instances where they are used, the practice conforms to the debtor's desires. Yet it is also clear that the lender can and does exert pressure if the need arises. The sale of secured property without the written consent of the lender subjects the mortgagor or conditional vendee to a criminal penalty.[43] Where the mortgage covers all of the property of the farmer, it is usually possible to find that some of that property, even if it happens to be just one cow, has been sold by the debtor. There is no question that lenders are very much aware of this situation and recognize a very effective remedy hovering in the background ready to be brought forward whenever necessary to bring a debtor into line. The exact extent of its use is difficult to ascertain, but there is no doubt that the threat of criminal action is used more often than the threat of formal foreclosure in the way provided by the civil statutes.

The methods by which threats of criminal sanction are used vary considerably. District attorneys interviewed were unanimous in saying that they did not like to have their office used as a collection agency and did not consider that, as public prosecutors, they were obligated to help collect private debts. Having said that, however, they also recognized that the criminal statute about selling mortgaged property is there. If the lender is willing actually to carry through to a criminal trial, the district attorney will take action.

The procedure appears to be that the district attorney writes to or calls in the debtor and informs him that the district attorney has been informed by the lender that the debtor has sold mortgaged property in violation of Section 343.69 and that a formal complaint will be signed by the lender unless some agreement is reached. The formal complaint is never signed, and the district attorney does not go through with the prosecution. All the district attorneys agreed that no jury would convict if it appeared that restitution had been made.

In the majority of cases, the district attorney never gets into the picture. The lender or his attorney may in the course of negotiations for settlement remind the debtor—presumably without threatening him—that some of the property is gone and that this probably involves the commission of a crime. Another very effective method is to serve a legal paper on the debtor in the form of a summons or a demand for return of the property sold. This generally has the effect of bringing the debtor's lawyer into the picture. In the interest of protecting his client from criminal action, he is coöperative, and it is not necessary for the lender's attorney actively to threaten criminal action.

One attorney reported that in his estimation the great value of the criminal provision is that the debtor's relatives will come to his rescue. Presumably the relatives are approached directly and the desired result reached. Suffice it to say that the criminal provision is there and is used effectively as a remedy for the lender. But it is difficult to get a clear picture of precisely what does happen because it is not a popular subject of conversation among the lenders who use it.

3. THE EFFECTS OF THE PROPOSED CODE

Under the proposed Uniform Commercial Code a lender has a right to the possession of the collateral when the debtor is in default. Presumably, right to possession before default by virtue of an insecurity clause is permitted if it is agreed to by the debtor. The lender may proceed to take possession without judicial process if this can be done without breach of the peace. Rendering equipment unusable is tantamount to possession.[44] A lender in possession is subject to the provisions of Section 9-208 relating to reasonable care of the goods.

It was noted earlier that the rights of the lender under existing law vary as to whether he has a chattel mortgage, a conditional sale, or a pledge agreement. The Code treats all lenders in possession alike, whether they have possession from the beginning, as a pledgee does under existing law, or only after repossession.

The lender in possession may sell the goods as they are or prepare them for sale by any commercially reasonable method.[45] The sale may be public or private, but every aspect thereof must be commercially reasonable. Reasonable notification of the intention to hold a private sale or of the time and place of a public sale must be given the debtor and any person having a filed security interest unless the collateral is perishable or threatens to decline speedily in value or is of a type customarily sold on a recognized market.[46] In most cases of farm chattels this would probably mean notice except perhaps in the case of crops which might be perishable or decline rapidly in value at certain times in the season.

The important considerations are, then, reasonable notice and sale in a commercially reasonable manner. If it appears that the lender is not proceeding in accordance with these provisions, he may be restrained or ordered to proceed on appropriate terms.[47] If the disposition has already occurred the debtor may recover any loss resulting therefrom. This appears to be a shift in emphasis from the present provisions for a statutory sale. Rather than setting up specific requirements of procedure with the background assumption that the lender will not proceed in the best interests of the debtor, the Code gives considerable discretion to the lender with the underlying assumption that the lender will act in the interest of the debtor. If he does not, the debtor has a remedy of restraint or actual damages.

The proceeds of sale are applied to the expenses and the indebtedness. The debtor is entitled to any balance and is liable for any deficiency unless otherwise agreed.[48] The lender may in lieu of sale, and unless consumer goods are involved, notify the debtor that he proposes to keep the property in satisfaction of the obligation. Within thirty days thereafter the debtor may insist on a disposition of the collateral. Procedure then is the same as if the lender had decided to sell originally.[49] At any time before the sale, a contract for sale, or the discharge of the obligation through retention of the property by the lender, the debtor may redeem by paying all sums due under the agreement, plus the expenses of taking and keeping.

In a comment on the provision for sale under the Code,[50] the draftsman indicated that although a public sale is recognized it is hoped that a private sale will be encouraged, since private sales through commercial channels will result in a better price. The emphasis on sale in a commercially reasonable manner is basic.

In this sense it is not too great a departure from present practice through the voluntary surrender. It improves upon this by requiring a reasonable notice of the proposed disposition of the collateral. There is also no doubt but that the public auction now used, insofar as farm personalty is concerned, would be recognized as a commercially reasonable manner.

The survey of existing practice would suggest as a matter of fact that a lender who, after enactment of the Code, followed present foreclosure requirements in disposing of the goods might possibly be held not to have disposed of them in a commercially reasonable manner. Certainly, all of the evidence gathered in this survey strongly indicates that lenders at least would not agree that the public foreclosure sale is commercially reasonable.

CHAPTER FIVE

Theory and effect
of existing law
# of chattel secured
farm credit

1. LAW AND PRACTICE

One of the very early principles of chattel security law was the prohibition against encumbering property to be acquired. The doctrine, apart from certain exceptions set forth by statutes, still exists in Wisconsin. The objection to encumbering such property is, in the language of the law, that "a man cannot grant or charge that which he hath not." Behind this reason there apparently is the suspicion that the debtor must be protected against the unscrupulous lender who will tie the debtor down for an unlimited period.

A second notable principle of existing security law is the prohibition against any freedom of disposition or exchange of the collateral in the hands of the debtor. This prohibition in effect denies the fact of a changing inventory in the hands of the farmer. The limitation is apparently designed to protect the lender against the ne'er-do-well debtor and to protect unsecured creditors against a conspiracy on the part of the debtor and the lender to defraud such unsecured creditors.

The third notable principle is the emphasis placed upon the out-of-court foreclosure sale. The requirement of notice and the provisions for making the sale public are theoretically designed to prevent the "unscrupulous" lender from taking advantage of the "down and out" debtor.

Behind each of these principles is a feeling that the parties to a secured transaction cannot be trusted to work out their own arrangement, that there will be overreaching by the creditor, and that there will be fraud on his other creditors by the debtor. Findings of this study show that such mistrust is not justified in the usual case. Although any system of jurisprudence to be effective must contemplate the unusual situation and be designed to meet it, in so doing it should not hamper or impede the normal situation. It is suggested that chattel security law does not meet this criterion and that there is, therefore, a need for a re-examination of its basic principles.

In making this examination, some attempt should be made to measure the real area of conflict in the chattel security transaction. For the most part, the principal doctrines noted above proceed on the theory that the real area is between the lender and the debtor. This survey, however, suggests that a feeling of mutual confidence exists between the lender and the debtor. The commercial institution, for example, places considerably more emphasis on its investigation of the background and moral character of the borrower than it does on the collateral. The question asked is whether the borrower is a good credit risk; if the answer is negative, adequate collateral will seldom produce the loan.

The real area of conflict, if we may believe the facts gathered in this study, is between the lender and third parties, and therein lies the value of the secured loan as against the unsecured loan. It is in this area that the doctrines operate to determine results, and here we might well inquire whether the results reached by existing law are in fact intended. The farmer has a constantly changing inventory and must have one for a successful farming operation. The lender recognizes this and permits such changes. Do we really intend that as a consequence the lender should lose his secured rights as against a third party unsecured lender on the theory that such freedom of disposition is a fraud on the third party? Do we intend that the prohibition against encumbering after-acquired property should operate so that all creditors, secured or unsecured, should share in the farmer's assets, with the secured party taking that which was on his original mortgage and the unsecured creditor taking property acquired subsequently?

Even if these results were intended, we may ask whether they are being accomplished at the expense of seriously discouraging the use of chattel secured credit for farmers. If, from an economic standpoint, agricultural production will be fostered by flexibility in chattel secured transactions, cannot that end be achieved without denying protection to third parties?

It would appear that a system of adequate notice by which third parties are protected can be established without hampering the transaction itself. Such a result does not run contrary to the theory of security law in general. The law, by the very fact of recognizing and giving effect to secured rights, recognizes the need for the fostering of credit. Third parties, meanwhile, are protected theoretically if they have notice of the transaction. It seems reasonable to suggest that this theory should be extended to after-acquired property and to freedom of disposition if such practice meets the economic needs of our agricultural society.

This result has, of course, been reached in other fields. When the above-mentioned prohibitions obviously acted to deny financing of the merchants' stock in trade, the legislature authorized the so-called "inventory mortgage" but limited it to mortgages on stocks in trade.[1] Again, in 1951, the legislature passed the Factor's Lien Act which extended the concept of the "inventory" mortgage to all personal property held for sale.[2] The results of this investigation suggest that the concept needs to be extended to farm credit transactions.[3]

This investigation indicates also a need for a re-examination of the institution of the public foreclosure sale. The evidence indicates not only that it is not used but that there exists a concerted effort, apparently sanctioned by the parties concerned, to avoid using it. Since there exists a suspicion that is is not the best means of securing a fair price, we need a scientific determination of the correctness of that suspicion. The legislature, meanwhile, has apparently accepted in part the correctness of the suspicion. The Factor's Lien Act of 1951 permits an agreement for foreclosure other than by the prescribed method for foreclosure of a chattel mortgage. The provision for such an agreement does not exist in the chattel mortgage statute and the conditional sales act. Reason suggests that if such an agreement is valid for a factor's lien the same reasons for its validity would apply to a chattel mortgage or a conditional sale.

2. The Uniform Commercial Code

As has been suggested, this study has been aided by the comparison of existing law and practice with the proposed Uniform Commercial Code. The going ways of business have been compared and contrasted, on the one hand, with existing law and, on the other hand, with the proposed code. Some further general observations on the underlying theory of the Code are therefore warranted.

As has been stated previously, the data gathered in the course of this study indicated a confidence between the lender and the farm debtor. The Code seems to have its entire approach based on the fact that this confidence exists. Thus it abolishes the prohibition against after-acquired clauses, thereby waiving the supposed protection which existing law gives to the borrower in this respect. It permits freedom of disposition in the borrower, which freedom does not render the transaction invalid. This waives the protection which third parties supposedly have under existing law. Protection is, however, afforded to third parties by provisions for notice of the existence of the security interest.

The Code authorizes a sale of security in a commercially reasonable manner by the lender after default. Thus, instead of assuming that the lender will take advantage of the borrower, as present law does by its insistence on elaborate foreclosure procedure, the Code assumes that in the majority of cases the lender will act in the best interests of the borrower. Remedy is provided in case he does not.

The future advance clause criticized in an earlier chapter is a further indication of giving recognition to the existence of this confidence. It will be recalled that a lender under the Code has priority for all future advances regardless of when they are given. The Code is in these respects noteworthy. It recognizes that security transactions are a necessary part of our present day economy and that the law exists to give effect to the needs of society. The law is not and should not be an inflexible mold. The Code is noteworthy also for the extent to which it abolishes our present haphazard security law which makes results turn on the

name of the transaction used. Under existing law the conditional
sale has one result, the chattel mortgage another, the pledge a
third, and the trust receipt, the assignment, the bailment, the lease,
the cropper's contract have still other results. Should there not be
the same result when the intention of the parties is a security
interest?

In spite of this conscious effort to avoid conceptualistic thinking by replacing form with function, the draftsmen of the Code
have refused to transcend certain of the traditional barriers. They
have, for example, refused to consider the effect of criminal sanctions in commercial law, apparently in the belief that criminal law
is for the criminal lawyer while commercial law is wholly civil.
The fact remains that criminal sanctions are used to enforce private
rights, often improperly.

In appraising this study in the light of the final draft of the
proposed Uniform Commercial Code, it is notable also that other
objectionable features of the Code which appeared in early drafts
were eliminated as a direct result of the information gathered in
this study. By studying the going ways of business in the chattel
secured field and by relating them to the proposed Code we were
able to detect instances in which the Code provisions, though suitable for other businesses, were wholly inapplicable to the needs
of farm credit. For example, Part 4 of Section 9 relative to filing
provided that all statements of accounts were to be filed with the
Secretary of State. This provision assumed that the usual account
would involve intercounty or interstate transactions. This assumption was not true, as the usual farm milk account shows. It
was also very likely to lead to confusion because other transactions
involving farm operations were expressly limited to filing in the
county. The final draft, for this reason, excepts accounts arising
from the sale of farm products. This draft gives uniformity to filing
provisions when the collateral involves farm operations.

An early draft defined farm products as crops and livestock
produced in farm operations. It was noted that such a definition
would not include livestock purchased by the farmer. Under this
definition, answers to questions such as the necessity of filing, the
place of filing, and the right to cull the herd would differ, depending on whether the particular animal was raised or purchased.
There was no logical basis for distinction on that ground. However, in the final draft the defect was corrected by changing the

definition of farm products to crop and livestock *used* as well as *produced* in farm operation. Similar results will be reached where similar results are intended.

It is apparent, therefore, that investigations such as this have an immediate and direct application on the Code. An appraisal of the needs of our present economy and an examination of how our law meets those needs provides a useful guide to our legislators in law making and to our courts in law interpretation. If the law is to do its job in ordering community relationships, the legal rules must give expression to the patterns of action which are established.

APPENDIXES

NOTES

INDEX

THIS MORTGAGE, Made this..day of ...., 19............,

by (1) (2) ...., whose

Post Office address is.., R. F. D. No................, Wisconsin, as Mortgagor, (the term

"Mortgagor" shall include several Mortgagors, where there are more than one; and shall include a Corporation, if it be the Mortgagor), to

.... PRODUCTION . CREDIT ASSOCIATION OF ....

whose Post Office address is..., Wisconsin, a Corporation, its successors or assigns, Mortgagee,.

WITNESSETH: That the Mortgagor, for the purpose of securing the payment of the sum of

.... DOLLARS ($..............................),

according to the terms and conditions of the following described promissory note or notes, executed by the Mortgagor to the Mortgagee,
viz.:

AMOUNT OF NOTE	DATE OF NOTE	DATE DUE	RATE OF INTEREST
$............................	...., 19..........	...., 19..........	..............per cent.
$............................	...., 19..........	...., 19..........	..............per cent.
$............................	...., 19..........	...., 19..........	..............per cent.
$............................	...., 19..........	...., 19..........	..............per cent.
$............................	...., 19..........	...., 19..........	..............per cent.

or any other note or notes given hereafter as a renewal thereof, or in renewal of renewals thereof, and any and all advances or loans

which may hereafter be made, not exceeding $................................, or other liabilities of the Mortgagor to the Mortgagee, with interest at

the rate borne by such note or notes, does hereby grant, bargain, sell, assign and mortgage to the said Mortgagee the following des-

cribed property, all of which the above named Mortgagor(s) warrant(s) is owned by, and is now in the possession of said Mortgagor(s)

on land held by such Mortgagor(s) as..., and described as follows:...
....(tenant(s)—owner(s))

in Section.......................... Township.................... Range.................... in the County of ....

State of Wisconsin, to-wit:

1. An undivided....................interest in and to any and all crops of (describe crops) ....

now growing and visible and in existence as such crop or crops, or harvested, on the..described
....(above and/or following)
real estate, together with all hail insurance placed on, carried or received in case of loss, total or partial, on any and all crops covered

by this Mortgage, to-wit: ....

in Section.......................... Township.................... Range.................... County.....................State of Wisconsin.

It is agreed between the parties that upon the payment by the mortgagor(s) to the holder of this mortgage from the first proceeds of

the sale(s) of the 19.......... crop(s) of.. of the sum of......................dollars, the lien of this mortgage

on such specified crop(s) shall be deemed released and discharged; but without prejudice to or a waiver of the lien of this mortgage

upon any other personal property therein described.

2. All the following described goods, chattels and personal property (including livestock), to-wit:

CHATTEL MORTGAGE

No. _____

TO

_____

OFFICE OF REGISTER OF DEEDS

STATE OF WISCONSIN, } ss.

COUNTY OF................

Received the within instrument this........day

of............, 19........, at............

o'clock........M., and entered in Chattel Mortgage Book,

on Page........, as Document No............

.... Register of Deeds.

By.. Deputy.

CERTIFICATE

I do hereby certify that this is a true, complete and

correct copy of original mortgage filed of record in the

office of the Register of Deeds of the County of............,

State of Wisconsin, on

the............day of............, 19........,

under document or Instrument No............ Production Credit

Association of ....

(SEAL)

By.. Secretary-Treasurer.

Dated.. 19........

Appendix A. Chattel Mortgage Form

together with all increase of the above described livestock and specifically including all personal property of a kind similar to that or those hereinabove described which may hereafter be acquired, and all wool, before and after shearing, from any sheep described herein, or their increase during the life of this mortgage, and all additions, betterments and repairs made to or upon any of the personal property hereinbefore described, until the indebtedness secured hereby is fully paid.

3. Also the following feedstuffs, to-wit: ....bushels of oats; ....bushels of barley; ....bushels of corn; ....bushels of wheat; ....tons of hay; ....of................; and ....tons of silage.

The mortgagor covenants and agrees that the feedstuffs hereby mortgaged, or so much thereof as may be required therefor will be used solely for the purpose of preserving and preparing for market the livestock hereby mortgaged, and without prejudice to the lien of this mortgage on all thereof not so used.

All the above mortgaged property is to remain in the possession of the mortgagor, unless and until the same shall be taken possession of by the mortgagee, as hereinafter provided; and the mortgagor covenants and warrants that all of said property is free from all liens, charges and encumbrances of every nature whatsoever, and that the mortgagor has good and lawful right to sell, mortgage and convey the same as aforesaid, and will warrant and defend the title thereof against the claims and demands of all persons whomsoever; that the livestock described herein is all of the kind now owned by said mortgagor at said location, whether in excess of the specified number or not; and that the description, age, marks and brands thereof are as stated and that said marks and brands, are holding marks and brands and carry title, although said livestock may have other marks or brands.

Should any or all of the animals above described or any of the increase be or become infected with disease and be destroyed by order of public authority and the mortgagor become entitled to indemnity therefor from the State of Wisconsin, the United States Government, or other public unit or agency, or if any of said property above described be destroyed or damaged by any cause whereby the mortgagor becomes entitled to indemnity therefor from any third person, the mortgagor, for the consideration above named, does hereby sell, assign and transfer to the said mortgagee all such sums due from said State, public unit or agency, or such other third person, and hereby orders and directs that the same be paid to the said mortgagee upon presentation of a duly certified copy hereof.

The mortgagor covenants and agrees: (a) that he will give the mortgaged livestock due and proper care, feed, shelter, and attention; (b) that he will in a careful, husband-like manner tend, cultivate and protect the mortgaged crops, and will properly harvest, thresh, pack, prepare, protect and store the same for market; (c) that, if and when demanded by the mortgagee, he will at his own cost keep the personal property herein described insured against loss by fire, lightning, theft, tornado and windstorm, and the crops against loss by hail, in some insurance company or companies approved by the mortgagee for at least the amount of the sums secured hereby, with loss, if any, payable to the mortgagee as its interest may appear; (d) that he will pay all taxes heretofore or hereafter levied or assessed against the property hereinbefore described; (e) that on the default of the mortgagor in the performance of any of the foregoing covenants, the mortgagee may do or perform any and all of the acts herein required to be done, and it is specifically agreed that any and all sums paid out or incurred by the mortgagee for the procuring of feed or care for the mortgaged livestock, or for the sowing, planting, harvesting, threshing, packing, preparing and/or marketing of said mortgaged crops; and any sums paid out by the mortgagee in providing insurance and/or in satisfaction of taxes or other liens which have heretofore accrued, or which may hereafter accrue against said mortgaged property or any part thereof, shall be immediately due and payable from the mortgagor to the mortgagee with interest thereon at the rate as by the above described note or notes provided from the date of the advancement thereof to the mortgagee; and shall be added to the amount of money secured by this mortgage and shall be protected by the lien thereof.

The mortgagor agrees that, except with the specific written consent of the mortgagee, he will not attempt to, and will not, lend, sell, mortgage, pledge or otherwise encumber the property hereby mortgaged, nor will he suffer any liens to be created against the same.

The giving of this mortgage is not intended and shall not be construed as waiving, releasing or relinquishing any mortgages, liens, or other security, if any, which may have been given heretofore as security for the indebtedness on any part thereof herein described, this mortgage being given as additional security for such indebtedness.

If there be any security other than this mortgage for the indebtedness secured hereby, then upon default the mortgagee may proceed upon this and other security, either concurrently or separately, in any order it elects.

It is further agreed that the powers conferred by this mortgage are in addition to, and not in substitution for, the right of the mortgagee to foreclose this mortgage by action.

The mortgagor covenants that all checks or drafts delivered to the mortgagee for the purpose of paying any sum or sums secured hereby will be paid upon presentment, and that all agencies used in making collections thereof, including those agencies transmitting the proceeds of such items to the mortgagee, shall be considered agents of the mortgagor or anyone by or on behalf of whom payment is sought to be made.

No extension, assignment, or transfer of the above described note or notes shall be considered as a discharge hereof or waiver of any default hereunder. No delay of the mortgagee in asserting any right accruing by virtue of any default in any condition hereof shall be construed as a waiver of such defaults, nor shall any waiver of any default in any condition hereof be construed as a waiver of such condition or as a waiver of any other term or condition or right hereunder.

The mortgagor covenants and agrees that the proceeds of the above mentioned notes and of further advances hereby secured will be used only for the purposes set out in the mortgagor's loan application to the mortgagee.

All of the rights, privileges and powers herein vested in the mortgagee shall inure to, and may be exercised by, any subsequent holder of the note or notes, or any renewal thereof hereby secured and this mortgage shall be binding upon the heirs, executors, administrators and assigns of the mortgagor.

Where applicable, words used in this instrument in the masculine gender include the feminine and neuter, the singular number, includes the plural, and the plural the singular.

Provided, however, that if the mortgagor shall pay all of said indebtedness and interest and all advances or loans made hereunder, as above specified, then this mortgage shall be void; and it is hereby agreed that if default be made in the payment of said debt, advances or loans, or said note or notes evidencing the same, according to the terms thereof, or any part or renewal thereof, or if default be made in any condition or covenant herein, or any attempt be made to remove or dispose of said property, or any part thereof, or if at any time the mortgagee shall deem said debt unsafe or insecure, it is hereby authorized through anyone in its employ or by an attorney or agent, to enter upon the premises where said property may be, remove and sell the same at public or private sale, after giving to the owner(s) of the equity of redemption in such property so taken the notice required by law, and also after giving to any subsequent mortgagee(s) whose mortgage(s) is (are) duly filed, the notice required by law, and out of the proceeds retain the amount then

due and owing on said debt and for any advances, with the expenses attending the sale, including an attorney's fee of................Dollars; and should default be made in the payment of said promissory note or notes or any part of renewal thereof, according to the terms thereof, or if default be made in any condition or covenant herein, the whole of said debt shall become immediately due and payable without notice (any right to notice being hereby expressly waived) and the mortgagee may commence action for the recovery of the whole of said debt, or proceed to foreclose this mortgage, as above provided in case of default upon the maturity of the whole of the debt secured hereby; and the delivery of this mortgage to an attorney for the purpose of foreclosure shall be considered sufficient to make said fees due and payable, rendering to the mortgagor the surplus after the whole of said debt and advances shall have been paid, with charges aforesaid.

IN WITNESS WHEREOF the mortgagor has duly executed this instrument the day and year first above written.

Signed, Sealed and Delivered in the Presence of:

	(1) (2) ....(SEAL)
....	
	....(SEAL)
....	
(CORPORATE SEAL)	....(SEAL)

(1) If the mortgagor is a married man, his wife is to be named as a joint mortgagor in the space indicated, and she is to sign the chattel mortgage as a joint mortgagor.
(2) If the mortgagor is a corporation, insert corporate name in space indicated, and have the executing officer sign name and title below. Corporate seal to be attached and acknowledgment below to be executed.

STATE OF WISCONSIN,
COUNTY OF ....}ss.

On this................day of................, 19........, personally came before me
....President, and ....Secretary
of the above named Corporation, who are to me known to be the persons who executed the foregoing instrument as such officers and as the free act and deed of said Corporation by its authority.

My Commission Expires ....Notary Public, ...County, Wisconsin

Appendix A. Chattel Mortgage Form

Promise and Authority To Execute a Crop Mortgage

I, _____ . _____, whose post office address

is _____ _____, residing in the town of _____ _____,

County of _____, State of Wisconsin, in consideration of a loan of $_____ made to me by the

_____ PRODUCTION CREDIT ASSOCIATION of. _____

acting under the provisions of the Farm Credit Act of 1933, upon my application therefor, promise and agree to use the money so loaned, in trust, for the purposes stated in said application; and I further promise and agree that when any crop is growing on land hereafter described, now owned, possessed, leased, farmed, or cultivated by the undersigned, more particularly described as the (give full legal description) :

_____

_____

that I will execute and deliver to said _____ PRODUCTION CREDIT ASSOCIATION

of _____ _____, upon demand, in such form as the

said association may require, a valid, first mortgage on all planted or growing crops thereon to secure payment to the said association of the note to be given for the amount in which said application is approved, together with interest and advances made in pursuance to the conditions of said application and the acceptance thereof; and I further promise and agree not to execute or deliver any other mortgage or agreement, or to encumber said crop, or do any act which might result in a mortgage lien or claim upon or to said crop prior to said mortgage so to be executed and delivered to said PRODUCTION CREDIT ASSOCIATION, in accordance with the terms hereof.

I hereby authorize, appoint, and empower _____ _____

of _____ _____ with full power of substitution or any other person thereunto designated by the said PRODUCTION CREDIT ASSOCIATION, irrevocably as my attorney-in-fact to execute and/or to acknowledge, deliver, file, or record such mortgage in the event of my failure or refusal promptly to do so as provided hereinbefore.

IN WITNESS WHEREOF, I have hereunto set my hand and seal at _____ _____

_____, in the County of _____, State of Wisconsin, on the

_____ day of _____, 194_____.

Signed, sealed and delivered
in the presence of:

_____   _____ (SEAL)

_____   _____ (SEAL)

                                                                 (Signature of Wife)

STATE OF WISCONSIN   } ss.

COUNTY OF _____ {

On this _____ day of _____ _____ 194_____, before me, a notary public in and for said County and State, personally appeared _____ _____

and _____ _____. known to me to be the person or persons named herein and who executed the above and foregoing instrument and acknowledged that ____ he ____ executed the same as _____ own free act and deed for the uses and purposes therein mentioned.

IN WITNESS WHEREOF, I have hereunto set my hand and seal this _____ day of _____
194____

_____

Notary Public _____

(Seal)   My commission expires _____

Appendix B. Crop Mortgage Form

MILK CHECK ASSIGNMENT

To the Treasurer of _____

or to any other person, firm or corporation to whom I | we may sell or deliver milk | cream during the year of 195____

For value received you are hereby directed to pay to _____ of ____

_____ that part of the proceeds due me | us or which may become due for milk | cream

delivered or to be delivered to you or your factory during the year 195____, as indicated below:

_____

_____

Dated at _____ 195 ____

Accepted _____ 195 ____

_____

Signed in Duplicate

Appendix C. Milk Check Assignment Form

85

PLEDGE AGREEMENT (By Borrower)

KNOW ALL MEN BY THESE PRESENTS, THAT WHEREAS, the undersigned has this day delivered to, and deposited with.., of......................................., Wisconsin,
(Bank)
(hereinafter referred to as "Bank"), the following personal property...

....

....

....

NOW THEREFORE, for valuable consideration the undersigned does hereby admit, declare and agree that said personal property is and shall be held by said Bank as collateral security for the payment of all liabilities of whatsoever kind or description, now existing or owing or which may hereafter arise or accrue or be contracted or created or become due or owing to said Bank, directly or indirectly, from or by the undersigned, howsoever the same may be acquired by the Bank.

Wherever the term "liabilities" is used herein, it shall include all indebtedness, loans, drafts, overdrafts, endorsements, accounts, checks, notes, guaranties, and all other obligations of whatsoever kind or description, whether of the same or different nature, now existing or owing or which may hereafter arise or accrue or be contracted or created or become due or owing to said Bank, directly or indirectly, from or by the undersigned, howsoever the same may be acquired by the Bank.

The undersigned hereby grants to said Bank, or any of its officers, or any agent or attorney of said Bank, full power and authority to sell, assign, convey, transfer and deliver at any time, irrespective of whether any of said liabilities have matured or shall be due and payable, the whole of said property or any part thereof, or any substitutes therefor, or any additions thereto, at any Brokers' Board or private sale without advertisement or notice, or demanding payment, or giving notice of any kind to anyone, all of which the undersigned hereby waives, or at public sale at any time, irrespective of whether any of said liabilities have matured or shall be due and payable, and without demanding payment, which the undersigned hereby waives, and on such notice as said Bank, or any officer thereof, shall determine, and with the right of said Bank to be purchaser at said Brokers' Board or public sale, and after deducting all legal or other costs or expenses of collection, sale and delivery, to apply the residue of the proceeds of such sale or sales so made to or toward the payment of any or all of said liabilities as said Bank, or any officer thereof, shall elect, returning the overplus, if any, to the undersigned.

Said Bank is released from all obligations or duty to collect or protect said pledged property, or to act upon any notice in reference to said pledged property or to present said pledged property for payment, or to bind or hold any maker, acceptor, endorser, or guarantor thereof, or to effect presentment, demand, protest or notice of non-payment with respect thereto, all of which the undersigned waives. Said Bank at any time may enforce collection of all amounts due or payable on said pledged property by suit or otherwise, and surrender, release, renew, extend or exchange all or any part thereof, or compromise any indebtedness evidenced thereby, and may apply the proceeds received from any of said property, and interest or other income received from any of said property toward the payment of any or all of the said liabilities, whether due or not. Provided, however, that the Bank shall be under no duty or obligation to sell said collateral or any part thereof or to otherwise enforce any rights with respect thereto. Said Bank at any time, and from time to time, is hereby authorized to have any securities, stocks, or bonds pledged hereunder transferred into its name or into the name of its nominee, without disclosing, if said Bank so desires, that such securities so transferred are pledged or hypothecated, and without any indication, if said Bank so desires, on any new certificate or other document issued to evidence such securities or any thereof, that such securities are pledged or hypothecated, and any corporation or association, or any of the managers or trustees of any trust issuing any of said securities, or their transfer agent, shall not be bound to inquire in the event that said Bank or said nominee makes any further transfer of such securities or any thereof, as to whether said Bank or its nominee has the right to make such further transfer, and shall not be liable for transferring the same.

The undersigned hereby gives to said Bank a continuing lien on the deposit accounts of the undersigned from time to time in said Bank for the payment of any or all of the said liabilities, and authorizes said Bank at its election at any time to apply the balance of said deposit accounts and any indebtedness due or owing from said Bank to the undersigned whether due or not toward the payment of any or all of said liabilities mentioned above, whether due or not.

Said Bank may transfer and assign this agreement and deliver the said pledged property to the assignee upon the transfer, endorsement, sale or assignment of the said liabilities, and in such case this agreement and the pledge of personal property hereunder shall inure to the benefit of and may be enforced by the transferee, endorsee or assignee of the indebtedness, liabilities and obligations so transferred.

Said Bank need take no steps whatsoever to realize on the property held by it as collateral hereunder. Said Bank from time to time without notice may surrender or release all or any property held by it as collateral, and grant extensions of time of or renew any of said liabilities for which said property deposited as aforesaid is collateral security. Said Bank may subordinate any or all such liabilities to other indebtedness, all without in any way affecting the pledge of collateral hereby made.

The rights and powers granted or evidenced hereby shall not be revoked by death of the undersigned and shall be binding upon the heirs, executors, administrators and successors of the undersigned, and shall continue in force after the death of the undersigned, and shall be applicable to all renewals and/or extensions of the notes and liabilities for which the property deposited as aforesaid is collateral security.

Signed and
Sealed at.., Wisconsin, this............day of......................................, 19..........

....(SEAL)

....(SEAL)

W.B.A. 156—'45
(REVISED)

Appendix D. Pledge Agreement Form

NOTES

Chapter 1

1 In the interest of simplicity at this point, I ask the reader to accept this statement at face value even though it does open questions of equitable title in the lender, legal title in the borrower, and right of a purchaser of the legal title over the equitable rights of the lender. Wisconsin is apparently committed to the theory that a chattel mortgagee gets legal title, although in *Midland National Bank & Trust Co.* v. *Peterson,* 229 Wis. 19, 281 N.W. 683 (1938), the court said that a chattel mortgage was for all practical purposes a mere lien. Thus in making this statement I am taking the position that the borrower has passed legal title to the lender by the chattel mortgage. As such, the rights of a second lender or subsequent purchaser would not rise above those of the first lender in the absence of a statute changing the rule of priorities.

2 7 Wis. 138 (1858).

3 1 Barb. 542 (N.Y. Sup. Ct. 1847).

4 8 Barb. 102 (N.Y. Sup. Ct. 1849).

5 10 Wis. 341 (1860).

6 1 C.B. 379, 135 Eng. Rep. 587 (C.P. 1845).

7 See *Blakeslee* v. *Rossman,* 43 Wis. 116 (1877); *Merchants' and Mechanics' Savings Bank* v. *Lovejoy,* 84 Wis. 601, 55 N.W. 108 (1893); *Franzke* v. *Hitchon,* 105 Wis. 11, 80 N.W. 931 (1899).

8 I suspected at the start of my investigation that the foreclosure provisions were seldom used but that the provisions for public filing

of the security interest was followed in every case. I was only par-
tially correct, as the reader will note from the discussion which follows.

9   See Note 1, above.

10 See Uniform Commercial Code, pp. 1–6 (Spring, 1950, Proposed
Final Draft, Text and Comments Edition).

11 Research for this study was begun at the time of the proposed final
draft of the Code. Naturally, the Code, particularly Article 9, as
well as existing law and practice dictated the approach to my material and established my method of presentation.

The reader will undoubtedly note that a favorite problem of personal property law—the problem of fixtures—is not discussed in
this study. This is not an oversight. I included the problem in my
plan for the study and briefed the law on the subject. When I got
into the field, however, I found it nearly impossible to elicit information on the subject. This may mean that it is not a pressing
problem, but more probably it means that the complexity of the
problem tends to cause avoidance of it. In any event, I received
little response when I posed the problem of the milking machine,
the milk house, and the stanchions. A possible explanation of the
lack of response is that there is a tendency to encumber all farm
personalty, often far in excess of the amount of the loan, and that
it is not unusual for the real estate and chattel secured loans to be
held by the same lender.

Chapter 2

1   Secs. 272.18(6), 272.18(15), Wis. Stats. (1951) exempt part of the
food supply from execution but not necessarily all that is needed.

2   See Appendix A for an example of the chattel mortgage form including an interest in growing crops. The wording of other forms
in use in Wisconsin is similar. One form requires the mortgagor to
mortgage, in addition to specified chattels, "all my interest in and
to any and all crops of every kind, growing or harvested, including
hay, grain, feed and roughage." Another provides "Also my undivided _____ interest in and to any and all crops of every kind,
including tame and wild grass and hay, which have been sown,
grown, planted, cultivated, or will be harvested during the year
19__ on the following described real estate . . . ."

3   See Appendix B for an example of the typical "promise to execute
a crop mortgage" form.

4   See Appendix B.

5 The language of a typical "crop mortgage with lease" specifies as follows: "Said first parties, if allowed to continue possession, agrees hereby to hold the premises as agent for the lessee."

6 *Comstock* v. *Scales,* 7 Wis. 138 (1858); *Merchants' and Mechanics' Savings Bank* v. *Lovejoy,* 84 Wis. 601, 55 N.W. 108 (1893); *Kohler Improvement Co.* v. *Preder,* 217 Wis. 641, 259 N.W. 833 (1935). Other states have recognized the validity of mortgages on crops to be grown on a theory of potential existence (an interest in the land gives the borrower an interest in the crops which can be the subject of a mortgage) or on the theory of an equitable lien (the mortgage constitutes a promise to give a mortgage; this can be enforced in equity and thus becomes a lien on the crop when the crop comes into existence).—See *Twin Falls Bank & Trust Co.* v. *Weinberg,* 44 Idaho 332, 257 Pac. 31 (1927); *Arques* v. *Wasson,* 51 Calif. 620, 21 Am. Rep. 718 (1877); *Wheeler* v. *Becher,* 68 Iowa 723, 28 N.W. 40 (1886). See also Comment, *Mortgages on Future Crops as Security for Government Loans,* 47 Yale L. J. 98 (1937).

7 *Chynoweth* v. *Tenney,* 10 Wis. 341 (1860).

8 *Ibid.* A lawyer in Northern Wisconsin assured me that he had successfully replevied property in reliance on an after-acquired clause. The case was not appealed. This attorney's explanation was that the judge simply decided to give effect to what the parties intended by their written mortgages.

9 *Id.* at 346.

10 43 Wis. 583 (1878).

11 Counsel here cited *Holroyd* v. *Marshall,* 10 H.L.C. 191, 11 Eng. Rep. 999 (H.L. 1861–62), the leading case on the equitable lien theory.

12 *Kohler Improvement Co.* v. *Preder,* 217 Wis. 641, 259 N.W. 833 (1935).

13 See the language of the typical "promise to execute a crop mortgage" form, Appendix B.

14 *Hunt* v. *Rousmanier's Administrators,* 8 Wheat. 174 (21 U.S. 1823); *American Loan & Trust Co.* v. *Billings,* 58 Minn. 187, 59 N.W. 998 (1894).

15 61 Wis. 153, 21 N.W. 62 (1884). See also *Manufacturers' Bank of Milwaukee* v. *Ruggee,* 59 Wis. 221, 18 N.W. 251 (1884); *First National Bank of Madison* v. *Damm,* 63 Wis. 249, 23 N.W. 497 (1885); *Smith* v. *Pfluger,* 126 Wis. 253, 105 N.W. 476 (1905). A Note, 1951 Wis. L. Rev. 175, discusses a similar problem of lease and bailment provisions in canner-grower contracts.

16 One agreement form in use states that "if a first lien chattel mort-

gage is executed upon the crops grown upon the lands hereinafter described, ... then and there the said trust shall be terminated without an accounting."

17   See Appendix B.

18   "... which said mortgage is to secure payment of _____ DOLLARS, to party of the second part."

19   See cases cited, Note 15, above.

20   Uniform Commercial Code § 9-102 (Nov., 1951, Final Text Edition). All references to the Code unless otherwise noted are to this edition.

21   *Ibid.,* § 9-109.

22   *Ibid.,* § 9-109(4). Crops are farm products while they remain in the possession of the farmer.

23   *Ibid.,* § 9-204(4)(a).

24   *Ibid.,* §§ 9-203(1)(b), 9-402(3).

25   See Appendix A. The wording of other forms is similar. For example, one form mortgages "all the following described goods, chattels and personal property (including live stock), to-wit: ... together with all increase of the above described live stock."

26   The wording of this form is as follows: "... all the following described goods, chattels and personal property, to-wit: ... together with any heifer calf or heifer calves to which said cows shall give birth."

27   See *Fowler* v. *Hunt,* 48 Wis. 345, 4 N.W. 481 (1880).

28   *Knapp, Stout & Co.* v. *Deitz,* 64 Wis. 31, 24 N.W. 471 (1885).

29   64 Wis. 35, 24 N.W. 419 (1885).

30   *Id.* at 40, 24 N.W. at 421.

31   As, for example, in the form shown in Appendix A.

32   *Cahoon* v. *Miers,* 67 Md. 573, 11 Atl. 278 (1887).

33   See *Brown* v. *Schwab,* 27 Ariz. 457, 233 Pac. 593, 39 A.L.R. 150 (1925).

34   Uniform Commercial Code § 9-110.

35   The interest attaches when the debtor has rights in the collateral. —*Ibid.,* § 9-204(1).

36   See Appendix A.

37   Even then it is not unusual for the bank to refinance the purchase with a chattel mortgage agreement after a few installments have been paid.

38   The bill of sale on the reverse side of the bank draft in the typical instrument has the following language: "That, in consideration of the amounts stipulated on the face of this draft, the receipt of which is hereby acknowledged, I (we) have bargained and sold unto

_____ at the risk and in the care of the signer of this draft, the property described on the face thereof and I (we) hereby warrant and agree to defend the title to said property against any and all persons claiming or to claim any right, title, interest or lien in, to or against the same or any of them."

39 Uniform Commercial Code § 9-102.

40 *Ibid.*, § 9-107(b).

41 *Ibid.*, § 9-102(1).

42 See Appendix C.

43 This acceptance is typically worded as follows: "We hereby accept notice of the foregoing assignment and agree to comply therewith as to any moneys or credits belonging to the assignor coming within our control, and we hereby agree that we will purchase, at the current market price, all milk (cream) from the said assignor's entire herd of cows during the term of this agreement."

44 This agreement is simply stated as follows: "The undersigned assignor hereby agrees that he will continue to deliver and sell the usual amount of milk and/or cream to the above mentioned Purchaser during the life of this contract."

45 The provision is usually written as follows: "In consideration of their mutual promises, the Seller agrees to sell and the Buyer agrees to buy, at the current market price at the time of delivery, all milk and cream from the Seller's entire herd of cows on his farm."

46 The language in one assignment form is fairly detailed: "That the first party does hereby sell and assign to the second party _____% of all claims and demands which the first party may now have or may hereafter acquire, against the third party now due or to become due for milk and cream so sold and delivered, or to be sold and delivered, in accordance herewith, and the first party does hereby order and instruct the third party to pay to the second party, to apply upon said indebtedness, any moneys due or to become due hereunder, such payments to be charged to the account of the first party, and the said third party does hereby accept such assignment and does hereby agree to pay said second party according to the directions of this assignment."

47 *Skobis* v. *Ferge,* 102 Wis. 122, 78 N.W. 426 (1899); *Cook* v. *City of Menasha,* 103 Wis. 6, 79 N.W. 26 (1899). For a criticism of the Wisconsin position, see Comment, 1939 Wis. L. Rev. 514.

48 *O'Niel* v. *Wm. B. H. Kerr Co.,* 124 Wis. 234, 102 N.W. 573 (1905); *Porte* v. *Chicago & N. W. Ry. Co.,* 162 Wis. 446, 156 N.W. 469 (1916).

49 Here again the assignment creates a revocable license in the lender

to collect the funds from the creamery. Yet the assignment has no provisions for right of entry, which is the basis for the revocable license theory in the chattel mortgage.

50 Sec. 241.09, Wis. Stats. (1951) prohibits assignments of wages for more than two months in advance. The statute is not applicable, however, to the credit institutions which I have contacted. There is also doubt that the milk check is salary or wages.

51 Uniform Commercial Code §§ 9-106, 9-102.

52 *Ibid.*

53 *Ibid.,* § 9-204.

54 E.g., § 499.9, Code of Iowa (1950); § 185.08(4), Wis. Stats. (1951).

55 For a discussion of the issues involved, see Note, 1949 Wis. L. Rev. 800.

56 Uniform Commercial Code § 1-201(37).

57 *Ibid.,* § 2-107(2)(b). Also, under § 2-716 of the Code the canner will apparently be entitled to specific performance of his contract. The comment on this section in the Proposed Final Draft (Spring, 1950, Text and Comments Edition) recognizes that output and requirement contracts involving a particular or peculiarly available source or market constitute the typical specific performance situation.

58 The problem of the pledging practices discovered in the course of this study relates principally to the rights of third parties and remedies of the pledgee. The practices only are introduced at this point; the law and Code provisions are discussed in Chapters III and IV.

59 See Appendix D.

60 In making this statement I am not overlooking the fact that the Federal government does make extensive use of a device which incorporates both chattel mortgage and pledge requirements in its price support program. Since the crop is sealed in a crib or warehouse, this program comes close to a field-warehousing arrangement. But this is essentially a price support program which finances agriculture only incidentally, and as such it is outside the scope of this study.

61 The chattel mortgage clause in such an agreement reads as follows: "That he hereby, to secure payment of said rent, performance of all convenants herein contained, and payment of all advances by said lessor, if any, MORTGAGES to said lessor, his heirs and legal representatives, all crops which shall be grown on said land each year; and in case of default in any of the covenants herein contained, he HEREBY AUTHORIZES and EMPOWERS said lessor, his heirs, or legal representatives, to cancel this lease, to re-enter upon

said land and take full possession thereof and of all crops then thereon, to foreclose said mortgage, to sell all such crops in manner provided by law for foreclosure of chattel mortgages, and, out of the proceeds of such sales, to pay all costs of taking possession of the same, foreclosing such mortgage and making such sales, to retain and pay all rents due hereunder. . . ."

62 For a discussion of the questions of ownership, see J. H. Beuscher, *Farm Law in Wisconsin* (1951), Ch. 9.

63 Such provisions are stated as follows: "That each party owns an undivided one-half interest in all of the _____ except as follows: . . . . That there are no agreements either oral or written between the parties hereto that prohibit either party from giving a prior lien or a first mortgage on his individual interest in the personal property mentioned above, and that neither party has or will assert a present or contingent lien or claim against the other party's individual interest in said chattels, or in the increase of any part thereof, which shall be prior or paramount to any liens of the Lender on the Property above described. That, if the applicant fails to pay his note or notes to the holder thereof . . . according to the terms of the mortgage . . . a division of the property shall be made by the Holder and the second party . . . that, upon such division, neither party hereto shall have any ownership interest in the respective halves set aside to each, and that part of the property set apart to the Applicant or the Holder shall alone be security for the applicant's debt and the costs and expenses of such division."

64 *Kohler Improvement Co.* v. *Preder,* 217 Wis. 641, 259 N.W. 833 (1935).

65 *Layng* v. *Stout,* 155 Wis. 553, 145 N.W. 227 (1914).

66 The statement that reservation of title is effective needs no qualification as between the parties. As to third parties, however, it may be ineffective because of an implied authority in the tenant to sell the crops. This possibility will be discussed more fully in the following chapter.

67 *Herreid* v. *Broadhead,* 211 Wis. 512, 248 N.W. 470 (1933); *Atwood* v. *Freund,* 219 Wis. 358, 263 N.W. 180 (1935).

68 Uniform Commercial Code §§ 9-102, 9-105(f).

69 *Ibid.,* § 9-204(4)(a).

Chapter 3

1 The exceptions discovered were one of the large finance companies and the time credit department of a metropolitan bank. These two

institutions carried an insurance policy which protected them against loss resulting from failure to file.

2   See §§ 241.08, 122.05, Wis. Stats. (1951). Both the chattel mortgage and the conditional sales contract are invalid against third parties who do not have notice of the lender's interest. Notice may be actual (knowledge of the facts, however gained) or constructive (opportunity to learn the facts by virtue of the public record). Prior to the 1949 amendment to § 241.08, the chattel mortgage was invalid as against third parties even though they had actual notice. Possession had to be delivered to the mortgagee or a copy had to be filed in order for the mortgagee to be protected. See *Graham* v. *Perry*, 200 Wis. 211, 228 N.W. 135 (1929) which compares the effect of §§ 241.08 and 241.11 (affidavit of renewal).

3   See Appendix A.

4   64 Wis. 31, 24 N.W. 471 (1885).

5   See Appendix A.

6   *Franzke* v. *Hitchon*, 105 Wis. 11, 80 N.W. 931 (1899).

7   *Southern Wisconsin Acceptance Co.* v. *Paull*, 192 Wis. 548, 213 N.W. 317 (1927). For similar holdings in other jurisdictions see *Abbeville Live Stock Co.* v. *Walden*, 209 Ala. 315, 96 So. 237 (1923); *Partridge* v. *Minn. & D. Elevator Co.*, 75 Minn. 496, 78 N.W. 85 (1899).

8   *Carr* v. *Brawley*, 34 Okla. 500, 125 Pac. 1131 (1912); *Ross* v. *State Bank of Trego*, 198 Wis. 335, 224 N.W. 114, 73 A.L.R. 225 (1929). Much of the case authority on this question relates to the stock in trade mortgage. Sec. 241.14, Wis. Stats. (1951) now regulates the stock in trade mortgage. The statute has no application to the farm transaction with which this discussion is concerned.

9   Uniform Commercial Code §§ 9-204(1), 9-204(2)(a).

10   *Ibid.*, §§ 9-301, 9-302.

11   For the requisites of a financing statement see *Ibid.*, § 9-402. In the case of crops, the land on which the crops are growing must be described.

12   *Ibid.*, § 9-303(1)(a).

13   See Robert S. Hunt and Glenn R. Coates, *The Impact of the Secured Transaction Article on Commercial Practices with Respect to Agriculture*, 16 Law & Contemp. Prob., 165, 169 (1951).

14   Actually, there is some doubt in my mind as to the validity of this conclusion. Both *A* and *B* would be claiming the crop under an after-acquired clause necessarily. This may take it outside the provisions of exception (4) which refers to a conflict between a purchase lender and a claimant under an after-acquired clause. This indicates to me again that the draftsmen did not consider the possi-

bility of a purchase money interest where the collateral is after-acquired.

15 Uniform Commercial Code § 9-205.

16 *Ibid.*, § 9-306(1).

17 *Ibid.*, §§ 9-306(1), 9-303(2), and 9-307 relative to buyers in ordinary course of business are not applicable. A buyer in ordinary course does not include one who buys from a farmer.—§ 1-201(9).

18 Hunt and Coates, 16 Law & Contemp. Prob., 171 (1951).

19 Sec. 9-307 is no longer applicable to the question of proceeds so far as the farmer is concerned. See Note 17, above.

20 Uniform Commercial Code § 9-205.

21 One form in use is an application by the debtor for a release of certain chattels coupled with a promise to apply the proceeds of the sale on the principal of the note held by the lending institution. Another form provides for additional chattels to replace the item or items released from the mortgage.

22 The language of the "supplemental chattel mortgage" is specific, as the following example will show: "This mortgage is intended to be supplementary to the aforesaid mortgage and to constitute additional security for all indebtedness secured thereby. The principal indebtedness and interest thereon secured by this mortgage, is evidenced by notes signed by the Mortgagor, as maker, and payable to the order of the Mortgagee, as payee, each of which bears interest in accordance with the terms thereof. This mortgage is intended to secure, in addition to said notes, any note or notes given hereafter as a renewal thereof, or in renewal of renewals thereof, and any note or notes evidencing advances, readvances, and loans which may hereafter be made by the Mortgagee to the Mortgagor from time to time within the principal sum secured by this mortgage together with interest thereon."

23 Sec. 241.14, Wis. Stats. (1951).

24 *Ibid.*, § 241.145.

25 *Bank of Baraboo* v. *Prothero*, 215 Wis. 552, 255 N.W. 126 (1934).

26 *Paine* v. *Benton*, 32 Wis. 491 (1873); *Schwenker* v. *Johnson*, 198 Wis. 300, 224 N.W. 117 (1929).

27 64 Wis. 35, 24 N.W. 419 (1885).

28 The practice was discussed in Chapter II under Security in Livestock.

29 64 Wis. 35, 42 (1885).

30 Emphasis supplied.

31 Sec. 241.08, Wis. Stats. (1951). The statute in effect when the case was decided was § 2313, Rev. St. (1878), which uses the same language.

32   See Note 2, above.

33   *National Bank of Commerce of Milwaukee* v. *Brogan*, 214 Wis. 378, 253 N.W. 385 (1934).

34   See 1 Jones, *Chattel Mortgages and Conditional Sales* § 81 (6th ed., Bowers, 1933).

35   Uniform Commercial Code § 9-313.

36   *Ibid.,* § 9-205.

37   *Ibid.,* § 9-307(2).

38   Compare the earlier remarks about the granting of such freedom in crop mortgages where the sale of the crop is the source of repayment.

39   See cases cited, Notes 7, 8, above.

40   This provision in one of the forms in use is fairly full and complete: "Should any or all of the animals above described or any of the increase be or become infected with disease and be destroyed by order of public authority and the mortgagor become entitled to indemnity therefor from the State of Wisconsin, or other public unit or agency, or if any of said property above described be destroyed or damaged by any cause whereby the mortgagor becomes entitled to indemnity therefor from any third person, the mortgagor, for the consideration above named, does hereby sell, assign and transfer to the said mortgagee all such sums due from said State, public unit or agency, or such other third person, and hereby orders and directs that the same be paid to the said mortgagee upon presentation of a duly certified copy hereof."

     Scott v. *Judd*, 255 Ill. App. 558 (1929), held that in the absence of agreement the lien of the mortgage did not extend to proceeds of indemnity.

41   See *Manufacturers' Bank of Milwaukee* v. *Rugee*, 59 Wis. 221, 18 N.W. 251 (1884); *Smith* v. *Pfluger*, 126 Wis. 253, 105 N.W. 476 (1905).

42   See *Southern Hardware & Supply Co.* v. *Clark*, 201 Fed. 1 (5th Cir. 1912).

43   See William F. Star, *Conditional Sales and Chattel Mortgages*, 9 Wash. L. Rev. 143, 143–145 (1934).

44   *Commercial Credit Co.* v. *National Credit Co.*, 143 Wash. 253, 255 Pac. 104 (1927). Most conditional sales contracts are in fact assigned to credit agencies and the agencies furnish the forms.

45   Uniform Commercial Code § 9-302(c).

46   *Ibid.,* 9-307(2).

47   Sec. 185.08(4), Wis. Stats. (1951).

48   See *Glassbrenner* v. *Groulik*, 110 Wis. 402, 85 N.W. 962 (1901). Compare *Curtice Bros. Co.* v. *Catts*, 72 N.J. Eq. 831, 66 Atl. 935 (1907). See also 5 Williston, *Contracts* § 1419 (rev. ed. 1937).

49 *Sedgwick* v. *Blanchard,* 170 Wis. 121, 174 N.W. 459 (1919); *Clay* v. *Woodrum,* 45 Kan. 116, 25 Pac. 619 (1891).

50 Sec. 241.28, Wis. Stats. (1951) contemplates an assignment as security for an obligation and defines account receivable to include amounts due or to become due under an existing contract.

51 Walsh, *Equity* § 62 (1930).

52 *Starks* v. *Redfield,* 52 Wis. 349, 9 N.W. 168 (1881).

53 *Taylor* v. *Collins,* 51 Wis. 123, 8 N.W. 22 (1881).

54 See A. L. I. Restatement, Torts § 943 (1939).

55 *O'Niel* v. *Wm. B. H. Kerr Co.,* 124 Wis. 234, 102 N.W. 573 (1905).

56 See *Benedict* v. *Ratner,* 268 U.S. 353, 45 Sup. Ct. 566, 69 L. Ed. 991 (1925), which recognizes this notion but holds the assignment invalid because of unrestricted freedom of use in the assignor. See also 4 *Corbin on Contracts* § 874 (1951), where the question is one of policy.

57 Uniform Commercial Code § 9-302(e). The assignment will be for financing and will affect a significant part of the farmer's accounts or contract rights.

58 *Ibid.,* § 9-204(2)(d).

59 *Ibid.,* § 9-312(3).

60 *Ibid.,* § 9-106.

61 *Ibid.,* § 9-318(2).

62 *Union Trust Co. and Security Warehousing Co.* v. *Wilson,* 198 U.S. 530, 25 Sup. Ct. 766, 49 L. Ed. 1154 (1905).

63 For circumstances held not to create adequate separation, see *Security Warehousing Co.* v. *Hand,* 143 Fed. 32 (7th Cir. 1906), affirmed, 206 U.S. 415 (1907).

64 Uniform Commercial Code § 9-305(2).

65 *Ibid.,* § 9-204(3).

66 *Ibid.,* § 9-205.

67 This opinion was expressed by some warehousemen at a conference on the Code at the University of Chicago, December 9, 1950.

68 Uniform Commercial Code § 9-305(1).

69 *Ibid.,* § 9-207.

70 155 Wis. 553, 145 N.W. 227 (1914).

71 *Id.* at 557, 145 N.W. at 229.

72 See the effect of freedom in the mortgagor to sell crops, previously discussed in Chapter III, Security in Crops.

73 There was evidence that over a course of years the lessors had permitted tenants to sell. The court then stated that an owner of property in possession of another might so act as to estop himself from claiming against a bona fide purchaser.—*Layng* v. *Stout,* 155 Wis. 553, 557, 145 N.W. 227, 229 (1914).

74 Sec. 241.03, Wis. Stats. (1951).

75   One such loss was against a mortgagee of the tenant's interest; another was against a purchaser of one-half of the crop from the tenant. Under the wording of the statute actual notice of the contract on the part of the third party does not aid the landlord.

76   Uniform Commercial Code § 9-312(6).

77   See Appendix A.

78   In language such as the following: "... and interest according to the conditions of the following described note or notes, viz.: ... or any other note or notes given hereafter as a renewal hereof, together with all advances, moneys, goods, credits, guaranties or overdrafts advanced or to be advanced to me or for me by within named Mortgagee."

79   In the insurance coverage issued to turkey growers there is a provision which states: "In the event of loss, this insurance company's liability shall be limited to the cost of the poults plus, from date of purchase, $1\frac{1}{4}$ ¢ per day for the first 60 days, $1\frac{3}{4}$ ¢ per day for the next 60 days and, thereafter, $2\frac{1}{4}$ ¢ per day until a maximum value of $4.00 per turkey is reached, which value shall be the maximum liability of this insurance company." Presumably, this standard is followed by the bank in its advances.

80   *Carter* v. *Rewey*, 62 Wis. 552, 22 N.W. 129 (1885); *Shores* v. *Doherty*, 65 Wis. 153, 26 N.W. 577 (1886).

81   *Davis* v. *Carlisle*, 142 Fed. 106 (8th Cir. 1905); *Freye* v. *Bank of Illinois*, 11 Ill. 367 (1849); *Boswell* v. *Goodwin*, 31 Conn. 74, 81 Am. Dec. 169 (1862); *Whelan* v. *Exchange Trust Co.*, 214 Mass. 121, 100 N.E. 1095 (1913); *Elmendorf-Anthony Co.* v. *Dunn*, 10 Wash.2d 29, 116 P.2d 253, 138 A.L.R. 558 (1941). See also 1 Jones, *Chattel Mortgages and Conditional Sales* § 97 (6th ed., Bowers, 1933); Recent Cases, 14 Min. L. Rev. 695 (1930); Albert P. Jones, *Mortgages Securing Future Advances*, 8 Tex. L. Rev. 371 (1930).

82   Compare *Elmendorf-Anthony Co.* v. *Dunn*, 10 Wash.2d 29, 116 P.2d 253, 138 A.L.R. 558 (1941).

83   *Whelan* v. *Exchange Trust Co.*, 214 Mass. 121, 100 N.E. 1095 (1913) (held obligatory where the full amount was credited to the debtor's account).

84   Uniform Commercial Code § 9-402.

85   *Ibid.*, § 9-204(5).

86   *Ibid.*, § 9-312(2).

Chapter 4

1   See Appendix D.

2   See Brown, *Personal Property* § 133 (1936); *Bank of the Old Dominion* v. *Dubuque & Pacific Ry. Co.*, 8 Iowa 277, 74 Am. Dec. 302

(1859); *Goldsmidt* v. *First Methodist-Episcopal Church*, 25 Minn. 202 (1878); *Linker* v. *Batavian National Bank of La Crosse*, 244 Wis. 459, 12 N.W.2d 721 (1944).

3 *Wilkes* v. *Allegan Fruit & Produce Co.*, 233 Mich. 215, 206 N.W. 483 (1925).

4 See *Robinson* v. *Hurley*, 11 Iowa 410, 79 Am. Dec. 497 (1861); *Wilkes* v. *Allegan Fruit and Produce Co.*, 233 Mich. 215, 206 N.W. 483 (1925).

5 *Frey* v. *Farmers & Mechanics Bank of Ann Arbor*, 273 Mich. 284, 262 N.W. 911 (1935).

6 *Linker* v. *Batavian National Bank of La Crosse*, 244 Wis. 459, 12 N.W.2d 721 (1944).

7 128 Ill. 533, 21 N.E. 510, 4 L.R.A. 586 (1889).

8 Notice the wording of this provision in one of the forms in use: "... the holder hereof has authority to sell all, or any part thereof, on the maturity of this note, or any time thereafter, or before in the event of said securities depreciating in value, in the opinion of the President, Vice-President or Cashier of said bank." Note, also, that the form shown in Appendix D has a provision for sale before maturity, whether or not there is a decline in value.

9 Brown, *Personal Property* § 133 (1936) (citing *Lucketts* v. *Towsend*, 3 Tex. 119, 49 Am. Dec. 723 [1848]; *Alcolea* v. *Smith*, 150 La. 482, 90 So. 769 [1922]).

10 *First Wisconsin National Bank* v. *Pierce*, 227 Wis. 581, 278 N.W. 451 (1938).

11 Seizure and sale may be commenced though the debtor is not in default. Most forms say that the lender may seize property when he deems the debt insecure. See *Hill* v. *Merriman*, 72 Wis. 483, 40 N.W. 399 (1888).

12 The junior mortgagee has no valid claim, however, unless he serves written notice of his mortgage on the first mortgagee. Thus, by § 241.13(4), Wis. Stats. (1951), if the first mortgagee does not serve notice on the second mortgagee and thereafter but before the sale the second mortgagee serves a notice on the first mortgagee, the sale does not cut off the rights of the second mortgagee. The only safe practice, then, is to serve on the second mortgagee or be prepared to postpone the sale.

13 Sec. 241.15, Wis. Stats. (1951).

14 *Ibid.*, § 241.134.

15 But see *Stierle* v. *Rohmeyer*, 218 Wis. 149, 260 N.W. 647 (1935) (held unconstitutional).

16 Except that the provisions regulating the procedure for a deficiency may be waived for consideration.

17   According to the provisions of this contract form, the lender "accepts the above contract and undertakes to perform all conditions thereof by it to be performed including the finding of a purchaser at private sale and the allowance of the 10% partial release of deficiency, all as therein stated."

18   Secs. 241.134(4), 122.221(4), Wis. Stats. (1951).

19   *Ibid.*, §§ 241.13(5), 122.26.

20   81 Wis. 566, 51 N.W. 1080 (1892).

21   Emphasis supplied.

22   93 Wis. 107, 67 N.W. 51 (1896).

23   See also *In re Davis Bros. Stone Co.*, 245 Wis. 130, rehearing denied, 245 Wis. 137b, 14 N.W.2d 870 (1944).

24   129 Wis. 125, 107 N.W. 1089 (1906).

25   See also *Stierle* v. *Rohmeyer,* 218 Wis. 149, 260 N.W. 647 (1935), which again concerned the penalty of forfeiture for failure to comply with the sale provisions. The court held the penalty provisions unconstitutional. The case involved a combination real estate and chattel mortgage. The chattel property was sold first and in violation of the statute. The mortgagor claimed that this satisfied the debt. The total obligation was $5000; the amount recovered on the sale was $260. The court considered this too penal. A note on this case appears in Recent Decisions, 20 Marq. L. Rev. 43 (1935).

26   Ch. 527, Laws of 1939.

27   Emphasis supplied.

28   205 Wis. 434, 237 N.W. 75 (1931).

29   129 Wis. 125, 107 N.W. 1089 (1906).

30   Sec. 241.13(3), Wis. Stats. (1951). Perhaps, also, if the amount of the remaining indebtedness is not particularly large, the court would deem it cancelled. See Recent Decisions, 20 Marq. L. Rev. 43 (1935).

31   *Mack International Motor Truck Corp.* v. *Thelen Trucking Co.,* 205 Wis. 434, 438, 237 N.W. 75, 77 (1931).

32   Where an auction company handles the sale, a new series of credit arrangements evolve with the purchasers. A conditional sales contract is used, though clearly the auction company is not the seller but a third party lender. The rationale may take two forms. In one, the auction sale agreement operates as a transfer of title to the auction company of all property to be sold. Then at the sale the contract is between the auction company and the purchaser. In the other, the agreement includes a power of attorney in the auction company to assign all contracts to the auction company. Here the contract is between the seller and the purchaser. A representative of the company then assigns the seller's rights to the company.

33   194 Wis. 29, 215 N.W. 433 (1927).

34   Apparently the auction agreement gives existence to the funds. Compare the milk assignment case, *O'Niel* v. *Wm. B. H. Kerr Co.*, 124 Wis. 234, 102 N.W. 573 (1905), which held that the funds in the hands of the creamery were subject to garnishment.

35   204 Wis. 393, 235 N.W. 794 (1931).

36   211 Wis. 648, 247 N.W. 857 (1933).

37   256 Wis. 395, 41 N.W.2d 299 (1949).

38   See also *Middleton Lumber & Fuel Co.* v. *Kosanke*, 216 Wis. 90, 256 N.W. 633 (1934); *Kramer* v. *Burlage*, 234 Wis. 538, 291 N.W. 766 (1940).

39   According to this provision, "in consideration of the premises aforesaid, the party of the first part does hereby assign, transfer and set over unto the party of the second part the sum of $_____ out of the proceeds from the sale of the personal property securing said mortgage, subject only to the expenses of such sale." Furthermore, "the party of the first part hereby ratifies and confirms all things done or to be done by the party of the second part and covenants that said mortgage shall at all times be and continue in full force and effect as to any and all property described therein which is not sold at the sale."

40   "Lienholder does not release, waive or relinquish his encumbrance or lien rights except to pass title to purchasers of said property at said sale."

41   The provision in this form reads as follows: "The sale to have the same force and effect and to operate as a regular chattel mortgage foreclosure sale, to all intents and purposes as though sold under regular chattel mortgage foreclosure except as to publication of Notice of Sale, which is waived, and the sale by usual posting, and public auction circulars substituted; making and filing of report of sale is also waived."

42   Compare § 511.11, Minn. Stats. (1945).

43   Sec. 343.69, Wis. Stats. (1951).

44   Uniform Commercial Code § 9-503.

45   *Ibid.,* § 9-504(1).

46   *Ibid.,* § 9-504(2).

47   *Ibid.,* § 9-507(1).

48   *Ibid.,* § 9-504(1).

49   *Ibid.,* § 9-505(2). In § 9-505(1) special provisions relate to consumer goods which vary in accordance with purchase price paid and waiver by the debtor.

50   See comment to § 9-504 (Spring, 1950, Proposed Final Draft, Text and Comments Edition).

Chapter 5

1   Sec. 241.14, Wis. Stats. (1951).
2   *Ibid.*, § 241.145.
3   I expect that the act is applicable in part to farm credit transactions
    —that is, to harvested crops held for sale. But it would not apply
    to the dairy herd since at the time of the agreement the cattle are
    not intended for sale.

INDEX